María José Lobo
Pepita Subirà

Top deck 2

MACMILLAN

Pupil's book

CONTENTS

Welcome to Top deck 2! page 4

Lesson	Page	Aims	Language	Skills
1 Volcanoes	**5**			
Introduction	5	Understand an email from a friend about their interests	Hobbies and interests School projects	**Read** and answer **Listen** and answer
Story: The last day of Pompeii	6	Understand a story about history Tell a story Read a poem	Volcano verbs Jobs	**Listen** and answer **Listen** and match **Tell** a story in groups **Write** the end of a story
About volcanoes	10	Understand a factual text Speak about volcanoes	Parts of a volcano, types of volcano, names of volcanoes	**Read** and find **Listen** and find **Ask** and answer questions
Language stop	12	Use the present simple of *to be* Use the present simple of other verbs	Excursions	**Listen** and find people **Read** sentences and work out rules **Speak** about what you and your classmates do
Do you know that ...?	13	Learn more facts about volcanoes around the world	Volcanoes Geography	**Listen** for special information
SKILLS TICKET	14	Read a legend	Families Legends	**Read** and answer – true or false **Project task: Write** an email to a friend
2 Art: Early modern paintings	**15**			
Introduction	15	Understand a letter in a magazine	School life Projects Art	**Listen** and answer **Read** and answer **Listen** and guess
Story: The early life of Paul Klee	16	Understand a story about a painter Speak about photographs Sing a song	Music Art School life and careers	**Listen** and match **Speak** about people in photographs
About early modern art	20	Understand information on a website Describe a painting	Art Art movements	**Listen** and match **Read** and answer **Speak** about a painter and a painting
Language stop	22	Use the past simple of *to be* Use the past simple of other verbs	Excursions Hobbies and interests	**Read** sentences and work out rules **Write** or **speak** about an excursion you went on
Do you know that ...?	23	Understand texts about famous painters and paintings	Art Museums	**Listen** and match **Speak** from notes about a painting
SKILLS TICKET	24	Find important information in a long text	Art Museums	**Read** and answer **Project task: Write** a letter to a friend
3 Ancient Egypt	**25**			
Introduction	25	Find places on a map Answer quiz questions	Rivers Maps Ancient civilizations	**Listen** and find **Read** and answer
Story: Pharaoh Hatshepsut	26	Understand a story about a pharaoh Use thousand figures	Ancient Egyptian life Daily routines Politics	**Listen**, guess and summarize **Tell** the story **Write** the story
About ancient Egypt	30	Understand facts about ancient Egyptian life Work out hieroglyphs	Rivers Pyramids Scribes and hieroglyphs	**Listen** and answer **Guess, listen** and check **Write** in hieroglyphs
Language stop	32	Compare things Ask questions with ...? and answer with	Rivers Buildings Adjectives	**Read** sentences and work out rules **Ask and answer** questions
Do you know that ...?	33	Learn more about ancient Egypt Summarize texts	Gods and goddesses Ancient Egyptian life	**Listen** and order **Read** and find meanings
SKILLS TICKET	34	Work out the order of a text	Explorers Discoveries	**Read** and order **Project task: Answer** quiz questions

CONTENTS

Lesson	Page	Aims	Language	Skills
4 Water on Earth	**35**			
Introduction	35	Understand the introduction of a project on water	Water, weather, environment	**Listen** and find **Listen** and answer
Story: A visit to a water project	36	Understand a story about mapping water in the developing world	Charity projects Water Technology Materials	**Listen** and guess **Speak** and summarize the story **Speak** about a photograph
About water on Earth	40	Learn about the water cycle Learn about global warming	Water Environment Geography	**Speak** about key terms in the water cycle **Read** and complete **Listen** and answer
Language stop	42	Ask questions in the present simple and past simple and give short answers Use adverbs of frequency	Doing a class survey Conserving water	**Listen** and find mistakes **Read** sentences and work out rules **Write** about how often you use water
Do you know that ...?	43	Learn about why we need water	Health Energy	**Listen** and choose the topic
SKILLS TICKET	44	Learn about an expedition	Explorers Geography	**Read** and answer **Project task: Write** part of a project and present it
5 Architecture	**45**			
Introduction	45	Understand the meaning of architecture, architects and other jobs Answer quiz questions	Jobs Building design and construction	**Speak** about your answers **Listen** and answer
Story: The Empire State Building	46	Understand a story about building a famous building	Building processes Building materials	**Guess, listen** and check **Tell** the story **Tell** a similar story from notes
About architecture	50	Learn about different types of buildings	Special features of buildings Skyscrapers Building materials	**Listen** for special words **Listen** and answer **Read** facts from a graph **Speak** about a graph
Language stop	52	Use *will* and *won't* to talk about the future Use adverbs of sequence	Building processes Future plans	**Listen** and find mistakes in pictures **Read** sentences and work out rules **Speak** about a new classroom
Do you know that ...?	53	Learn about the tallest and most interesting buildings in the world	Special features of buildings	**Read** and find
SKILLS TICKET	54	Learn about builders	Jobs	**Read** and order **Read** and answer **Project task: Write** questions, hold and write up an interview
6 Discovering New Zealand	**55**			
Introduction	55	Understand a travel guide about New Zealand	Geography Animals and wildlife	**Listen** and answer
Story: Captain Cook	56	Understand a story about the discovery of New Zealand	History Sailing Discoveries	**Listen** and guess **Listen** and answer **Speak** about a special subject
About New Zealand	60	Learn about the history, wildlife and sports of New Zealand	Politics Animals and wildlife Sports	**Listen** and answer **Read** and understand
Language stop	62	Use the present continuous Use the past continuous	Travelling Sightseeing	**Read** a diary **Read** sentences and work out rules **Listen** and answer **Write** about photographs
Do you know that ...?	63	Learn more interesting facts about the history and geography of New Zealand	Animals and wildlife Places of interest	**Listen** and find **Read** and answer
SKILLS TICKET	64	Learn about famous New Zealanders	Careers	**Read** and answer **Project task: Plan** a holiday to New Zealand and **make** a photo album

Top Deck Race page 65   **European Day of Languages** page 66   **Chinese New Year** page 68   **Earth Day** page 70

Welcome to *Top deck 2*!

Top deck 2 takes you on a journey from Pompeii in AD 79, via ancient Egypt and New York City, and ends in New Zealand. Each of the six units contains the following stops on the journey:

In the introduction, you learn the main topic and words of the unit and meet important people. You also get a task to prepare all through the unit which you do at the end.

Story
The story is the main focus of the unit. You learn all about an event, a project or the life of a person through looking at pictures, listening, reading and speaking.

About
Then, you learn all about the main topic of the unit: volcanoes, early modern art, ancient Egypt, water on Earth, architecture and New Zealand. These are all things that you learn in your other school lessons – history, geography, art, etc.

Language stop
Here you focus on the main language of the unit.

Do you know that ...?
On this page, you learn lots of interesting and fun facts about the topic.

SKILLS TICKET
Finally, you can practise all four skills: reading in your pupil's book, listening in your *Top deck 2 Activity book* and then there is a writing and/or speaking activity in the final project task.

You will find these symbols in your book:

1.01 When you see this CD, you can listen to a conversation or text.

Super Tour 1 When you see the Super Tour box, you can find extra activities. If you finish an activity early and need more work, look at the different choices. Some Super Tour boxes contain ideas for projects.

Learning to learn
When you see these Learning to learn symbols next to an activity, it gives you an idea of how to understand and find the answers. The big letter tells you which skill you are practising:

R$_1$ Reading **L**$_1$ Listening **S**$_1$ Speaking **W**$_1$ Writing

The number tells you which Learning to learn strategy will help you. You can find all of the Learning to learn strategies on pages 66–67 of your *Top deck 2 Activity book*. You can also find activities to train these strategies.

In your *Top deck 2 Activity book*, you will find extra grammar notes on pages 74–79 and both a unit-by-unit and A–Z word list from page 80.

1 Volcanoes

In this unit you will
- learn and give information about volcanoes
- identify personal pronouns and the present simple of the verb *to be* and other verbs
- use this knowledge to plan and write an email

1 🔊 1.01 Listen and read

✉ Volcanoes

File Edit View Insert Format Tools Message Help

📧 Send

From: Paola
To: My new friends
Subject: Volcanoes

Dear friends,

My name is Paola. I am 12 years old. I live in Naples in Italy. Naples is a city near the volcano Mount Vesuvius. I am interested in volcanoes. I think that they are fascinating. Are there any volcanoes in your country? I know about Vesuvius but I want to know more about volcanoes in general because I need to do a presentation at school. Can you help me?

Thank you very much.

Paola

PS I am attaching two pictures: Mount Vesuvius and Naples. I hope you like them.

① Mount Vesuvius is an active volcano. The last big eruption was in March 1944.

② Today about three million people live near Mount Vesuvius.

1 Story

The last day of Pompeii

2 🔊 1.02 **Look, listen and read**

Pompeii is a commercial Roman city. There are many rich people in Pompeii. Trading is very important. Today is 24th August AD 79. It is early in the morning and the sun is shining.

①

Marcus Cornelius is a rich man. He lives in a very big house with his wife and daughter. He produces olive oil and exports it. Today he is going to the harbour.

Goodbye, Cornelia. I'm taking some oil to the harbour. One of my boats is ready to leave tomorrow. Goodbye, Marcia. Be a good girl.

Yes, Dad. See you this evening.

②

Marcus Cornelius and his servants start the journey to the harbour.

③

Suddenly, the ground shakes and there is a big explosion. A high column of smoke appears in the sky. It is coming from the top of Mount Vesuvius.

We must go back home! Come on!

④

Marcus Cornelius is very scared. He calls his wife and his daughter.

Cornelia! Marcia! Let's go! Hurry up! The mountain has exploded!

⑤

Unit 1

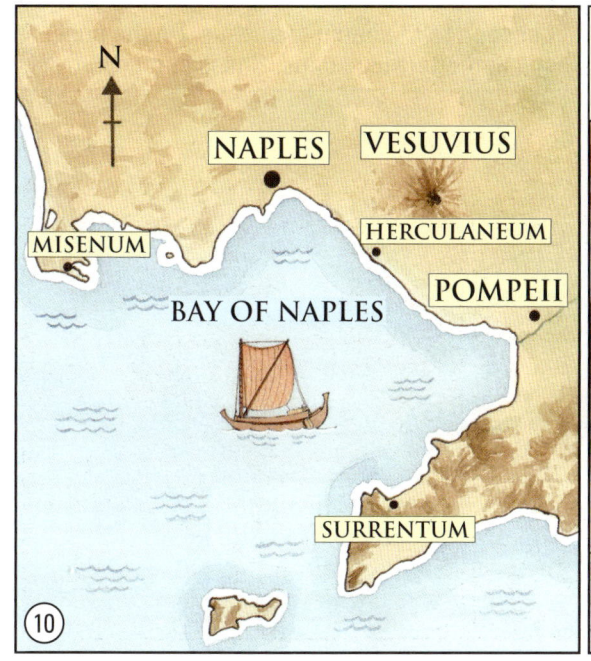

6. The mountain? But the ground is shaking. It's an earthquake!

No, it's the mountain. You can see it from the road. Look at the ash and smoke!

7. Quick! We must pack the gold and take some water and clothes.

There's no time to take anything! We must escape! Come on! Let's get out of here.

8. Come on, Cornelia. Stay close to me.

9. Let's go to the harbour. We can escape by boat and go far away.

Far away? But where?

We can go south to Surrentum or north-west to Misenum. Don't be afraid, Marcia. It's going to be OK.

10. N — MISENUM • NAPLES • VESUVIUS • HERCULANEUM • POMPEII • BAY OF NAPLES • SURRENTUM

11. The harbour is about two kilometres away. The situation is getting very bad. It is raining ash and stones. One stone hits Marcus Cornelius on his head.

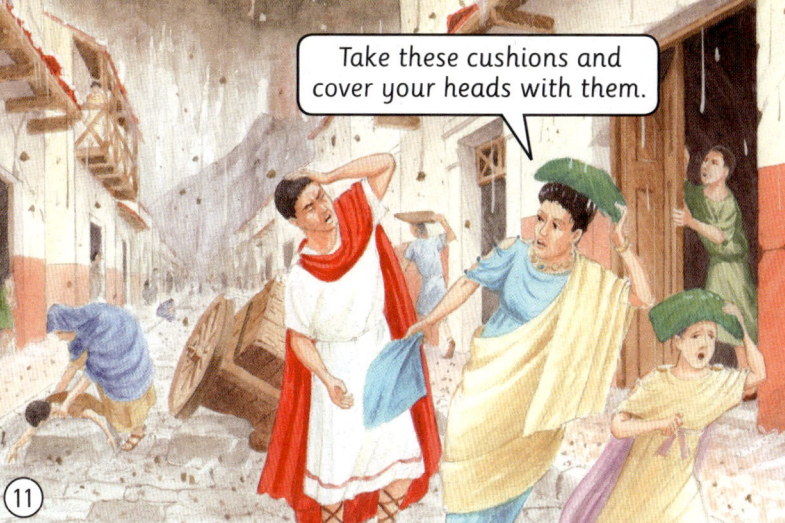

Take these cushions and cover your heads with them.

1 Story

12 There is chaos in the streets.
- My son! Where's my son?
- It's the end of the world!
- Help!

13 The air is thick. It is very hot and it is very difficult to breathe.
- I can't breathe.
- Cover your mouth with your cloak.
- It's impossible to get to the harbour. It's too far away.

14 It is 11 am but it is dark. A cloud of ash and stones covers the sun. The air smells of sulphur. It is almost impossible to breathe. Big rivers of lava run down the slopes of Mount Vesuvius.

15 Let's hurry up. We're almost at the harbour. The wind is blowing south. It's taking the ash to Surrentum. So we must go north-west.

16
- How can we sail? The sea is really rough!
- We must try. It's our only hope. Look! There's our boat!

17 The family must escape to Misenum to survive. On the boat, Marcia looks back at the terrible scene. She is sad and afraid.
- What's happening to our beautiful city? Why are the gods angry with the people of Pompeii?

Unit 1

3 Tell the story in groups

Super Tour 1

1 Write a different end to the story. Did the family escape? Did they go to a different town?
2 Think of ten things that happened to the Cornelius family when they arrived in Misenum. Who did they meet? Where did they sleep? etc. Tell your classmates.

4 🔊 1.06 Read the poem

What do you do when the ground shakes, shakes, shakes, shakes?
What do you do when the mountain shakes, shakes, shakes, shakes?
What do you do when the house shakes, shakes, shakes, shakes?

You escape, escape, escape!
You escape when the ground shakes.

Escape from your room!
Escape from your house!
Escape from your school!
Escape from your town!

You escape, escape, escape!
You escape when the ground shakes.

1 About volcanoes

1 🔊 1.07 **Read and listen**

Why volcanoes erupt

This is a pressure cooker. Steam escapes through a valve. A volcano is a pressure valve of the Earth. When a volcano erupts, excess energy inside the Earth comes to the surface. It pushes out through the crater of a volcano.

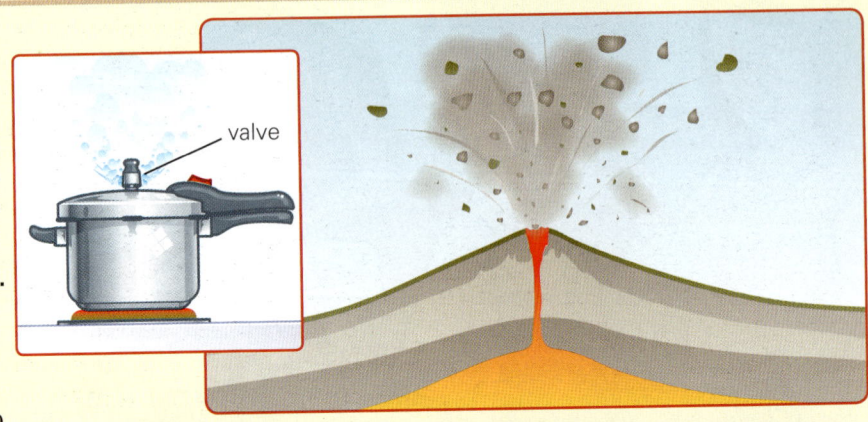

A cross section of a volcano

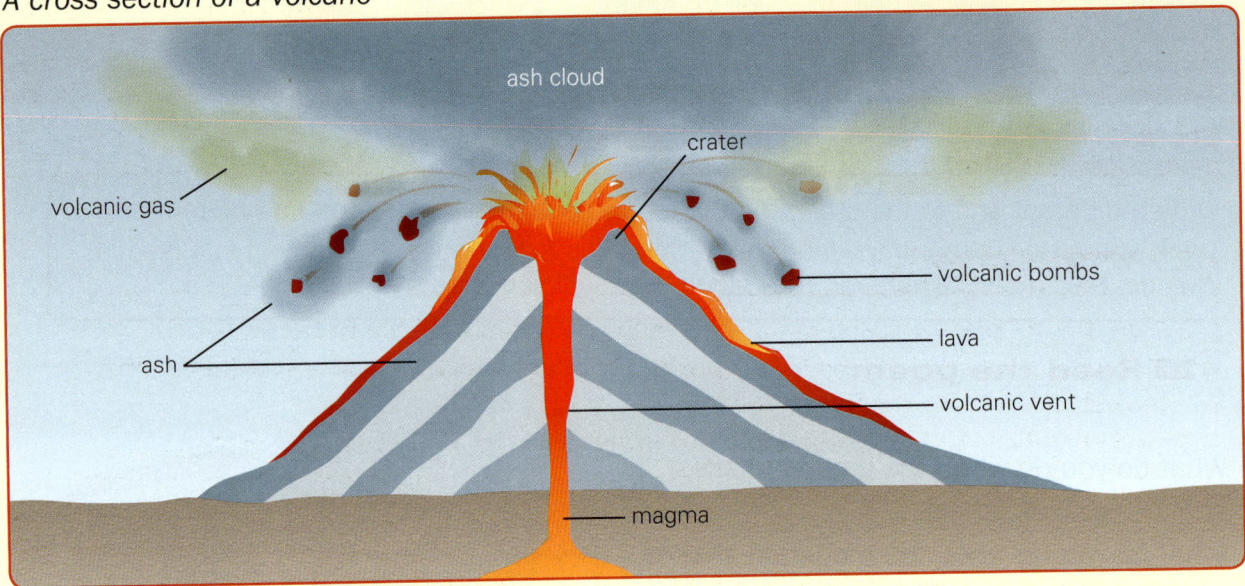

Magma is the hot molten (liquid) rock and gas inside the Earth.

Lava is the magma that comes out of the Earth in a volcanic eruption. Lava can be over 1,200°C!

Ash is pieces of lava or rock smaller than two millimetres in diameter.

An ash cloud is a cloud of ash formed by volcanic explosions.

A volcanic vent is the channel for magma to travel up towards the surface.

A crater is the mouth of a volcano around a volcanic vent. It is usually circular.

Volcanic bombs are rocks bigger than 64 millimetres in diameter.

Volcanic gas is the gas that goes into the atmosphere when there is volcanic activity. Some gases are toxic and can kill people.

Unit 1

2 🎧 1.09 Listen and speak

There are three different types of volcano:

① Active

Mount St Helens

The volcano is 'alive'. Eruptions are frequent.

Examples
- Mount St Helens in the USA
- Popocatépetl in Mexico
- Vesuvius in Italy

② Dormant

Teide

The volcano is 'asleep'. The last eruption was a very long time ago, but it may erupt again.

Examples
- Teide in Spain
- Mauna Kea in Hawaii

③ Extinct

Akaroa

The volcano was 'alive' many years ago, but after many thousands of years there are no signs of activity at all.

Examples
- Akaroa in New Zealand
- Puy de Dôme in France

🌀 Super Tour 2

1 Mark the different volcanoes in the examples on a map of the world.
2 Find some more volcanoes in the world. Mark them on your map and write whether they are active, dormant or extinct.
3 Find out which is the closest active, dormant and extinct volcano to where you live.

---

3 🎧 1.11 Listen and read

When the plates under the Earth's surface move, they sometimes crash. There is a lot of pressure under the surface.

There are more than 500 active volcanoes in the world. Many of these volcanoes are in the 'Ring of Fire' in the Pacific Ocean.

About 80% of the Earth's surface is volcanic in origin, including the sea bed and many mountains.

Geysers and fumaroles are also signs of volcanic activity.

Ring of Fire

Geyser

Fumarole

1 Language stop

1 🔊 1.12 **Listen and find the people**

Sandra   Helen   Richard   Laura   Mr Barnes   Peter   Joanna   Mr Smith

2 Read and answer

I **lead** the group.
You **teach** geography.
He **drives** the bus.
She **helps** on the trip.
It **takes** people to the volcano.
We **like** adventure.
You **go** to Greendale School.
They **study** geography.

1 Do you remember what happens to the verb when the pronoun is *he/she/it*?
2 Can you explain the rule in English?
3 Is there a rule in your language, too?

Super Tour 3

Say what you and your classmates do. Make sentences with *help*, *like*, *go*, *study*, *play*, *watch*, etc.

Do you know that …?

1 🔊 **1.13 Listen and read**

1 The word *volcano* comes from the name of Vulcan, the god of fire in Roman mythology.

2 There are volcanoes on land and under the sea. About 80 volcanoes under the sea are erupting now or will erupt in the next few years.

3 The Hawaiian islands, in the Pacific Ocean, are volcanic. Mauna Loa, on the island of Hawaii, is the largest and most active volcano on Earth. The last time it erupted was in March 1984. The Hawaiian name Mauna Loa means *long mountain*.

4 Most European volcanoes are on the Mediterranean coast. Santorini, on the island of Thira, erupted in 1470 BC and destroyed the civilization of Crete. Vesuvius, in Italy, erupted in AD 79 burying the towns of Pompeii and Herculaneum.
Mount Etna, on the island of Sicily, is the largest active volcano in Europe and one of the most active in the world. The last eruption was in May 2008.

5 Eolic is the name of a group of small Italian islands to the north of Sicily. All the Eolic islands are volcanic. The eruptions of Stromboli and Vulcano created the two beautiful islands with the same names.
Jules Verne is the author of the famous novel *Journey to the Centre of the Earth*. The journey begins at the volcano Snæfellsjökull in Iceland and ends at Stromboli.

6 There are 35 active volcanoes in Iceland, an island in the Atlantic Ocean. Eyjafjallajökull is one of those volcanoes. It erupted in April 2010. A large ash cloud went into the sky above Europe and planes could not fly over Britain, France, Germany, Switzerland and many other countries for about six days. There was chaos at many airports!

🌀 Super Tour 4

1 Make a mind map with the word *Volcano* in the middle. Write the headings: *Under the sea*, *Hawaii*, *The Mediterranean coast*, *Iceland* and use the information on this page.
2 In groups, find out more about one of the volcanoes on this page and create your own story about when it erupted.

SKILLS TICKET

1 🔊 1.15 **Read**

The legend of Popocatépetl and the princess

This legend comes from Mexico in the time when the Aztecs lived in the valley where Mexico City is today.

The Aztec Emperor Tizoc, his wife and their daughter, Princess Iztaccíhuatl, lived in a beautiful palace in the city of Tenochtitlan. Izta was in love with Popocatépetl, one of her father's soldiers.

One day Popocatépetl asked Tizoc for permission to marry the princess, but the emperor did not want Popocatépetl to marry his daughter. Then the emperor had an idea. He sent Popocatépetl to war with the promise of marrying Izta if he returned victorious.

Some months later, some soldiers returned to Tenochtitlan. They said that Popocatépetl was dead and that he died in battle. Izta was so sad that she died of grief.

It was not true that Popocatépetl was dead. When he returned victorious to Tenochtitlan, he was very happy. He went straight to the emperor's palace. There the emperor told him that Izta was dead. Popocatépetl went to Izta's grave and knelt at her side. The gods covered them with snow and changed them into mountains.

If someday you visit Mexico City, you will see the two beautiful volcanocs, one next to the other: Popocatépetl with Iztaccíhuatl lying at his side and always covered with snow.

2 Read and answer – true or false?

1 Mexico City is now in the valley where the Aztecs once lived.
2 Tizoc wanted his daughter to marry Popocatépetl.
3 Tizoc promised that Popocatépetl could marry Izta if he was a good soldier in the war.
4 Izta was very sad when she heard that Popocatépetl was dead and she also died.
5 Popocatépetl never returned victorious.
6 The emperor turned the soldier into a mountain.

Super Tour 5

1 Read the text again and find the words beginning with a capital letter.
2 Why are these words written with a capital letter? Write who/what they are, for example, *Mexico is a country*.

2 Art: Early modern paintings

In this unit you will
- learn about the life and work of some painters and give information about paintings
- use the past simple of the verb *to be*, regular verbs and some irregular verbs
- use this knowledge to plan and write a letter

1 🔊 1.16 **Listen and read**

Hi,
I'm Daniel. I'm a pupil in the sixth grade of primary school. In my school there are two sixth grade groups of 25 pupils. We are 11 years old. Our school is in Barcelona, Catalonia, Spain. This year we are doing a project in our English lessons about famous painters of the early 20th century. One of these painters is Pablo Picasso.

There is a Picasso museum in our city. We visited it last week and now we have some interesting information about Picasso's life and paintings.

Here are two photos of the museum. One of them shows the entrance. The museum is in a beautiful Gothic palace in the Gothic quarter of the city.

The other photo is Picasso's painting *Harlequin*. He painted it in 1917. You can see it in the museum.

We invite pupils from other schools to contact us and share information about their projects on painters and paintings around Picasso's time.

Is there an art gallery in your town or city? Can you send us information about it?

Thanks a lot,
Daniel

15

2 Story

The early life of Paul Klee

2 🔊 1.17 Look, listen and read

1. Hans and Ida Klee were musicians. Hans was a music teacher and he played the piano and the violin. Ida was a singer.

2. Hans and Ida lived in a village near Bern, Switzerland. They had a daughter, Mathilde. She was three years old when her brother was born in 1879.

- Look Mathilde, you've got a baby brother!
- Oh, a baby brother! What's his name?
- We're going to call him Paul.

3. In 1880, when Paul was one year old, Paul's father went to teach at a school in Bern. The family moved there.

- I like teaching in the new school and I think living in Bern is going to be good for us all.
- And my mother lives here and can help us with the children.

4. Young Paul often heard music at home. Hans played songs on the piano and the violin and Ida sang. Paul enjoyed this very much.

- Me too. And I like the music Dad plays.
- I love Mum's songs!

5. Paul's grandmother visited the Klee family quite often. She liked drawing. One day, she gave Paul some chalks. She taught Paul how to draw and colour.

- Grandma, look at my drawing. Do you like it?
- Paul, that's good. You're doing very well!

Unit 2

6. On Paul's seventh birthday, his parents had a special present for him.

- Wow! It's a violin. Thank you.
- Why don't you play a tune?
- I can't. I don't know how to.
- Let's try together. Just look at me.

7. So Paul tried to play the violin. His family saw immediately that he had talent.

- Not bad for the first time!
- He plays very well.

8. Hans began to teach Paul the violin. Paul learnt fast.

- Good, Paul. Well done!

9. Paul also continued to draw and he was good at that, too.

- Look at Paul's drawings. He draws really well now.
- Yes, they're great.

10. When he was 11, Paul started to play the violin with the Bern Musical Association. His father was happy. He wanted Paul to be a musician.

- It's fantastic that Paul is playing here. He's going to have a great future in music.

2 Story

11 But Paul's love of drawing grew, too. He decorated his school books with caricatures.

— These are very clever caricatures in your school books, Paul.
— Caricatures in your school books?!

12 — Yes, I draw caricatures. I also like copying drawings from magazines and calendars … and these are some pictures of landscapes.
— They're good, but please don't draw in your school books again.
— OK, Dad.

13 At secondary school, Paul started to think about his future.

— I love music and Dad wants me to be a musician, but I think about painting all the time.

14 It wasn't easy for Paul to decide what to study, but when he finished secondary school in 1898 …

— Dad, I want to study art in Munich.
— Why not study music? You're a good violinist!
— Yes, but I want to study art. I want to be an artist!

15 Paul moved to Munich in 1898. There he continued his journey as an artist. It made him famous all over the world.

— Goodbye, Paul. Good luck!
— Write soon!
— I will. Goodbye.

16 In April 1898, before he left school, Paul started to keep a diary. He wrote it until 1918. We can still read the diary today and learn about his life and his thoughts.

Unit 2

3 Who were they? Speak

I think …

He/She looks like …

I can see …

Super Tour 1

1 Look at the story of the early life of Paul Klee. Say a year and see if your classmates can tell you what happened in Paul's life.
2 What do you think happened in Paul Klee's life when he left home? Talk to a classmate.

4 🔊 1.19 Sing the song

I wanted to play music.
I wanted to sing a song.
I wanted to write a poem.
I wanted to draw the world.

Did you want to be a musician?
Well, I'm not sure at all.

Did you want to be a singer?
Certainly not!

Did you want to be a poet?
Of course not!

Did you want to be a painter?
Yes, of course!

I wanted to be an artist,
The best artist in the world!

2 About early modern art

1 🔊 1.20 **Listen and read**

| Home | Paintings | What's on | Visiting | Learning | Shop |

ART ONLINE

▼ Impressionism

Impressionism started in France around 1870. The Impressionists often painted outside, directly from nature. They tried to capture the immediate effect of light and colour at particular times of the day. They did not use black and they made shadows by mixing different colours. They mainly painted landscapes and scenes of daily life. The main Impressionist painters were Pierre-Auguste Renoir, Claude Monet and Edgar Degas among others.

Claude Monet (France 1840 – France 1926)
Poppies, 1873. Oil on canvas
Musée d'Orsay, Paris

▼ Expressionism

Expressionism started in Germany at the beginning of the 20th century. Expressionist painters wanted to express their feelings and emotions. They did not try to reproduce objects accurately. There were two main German Expressionist groups:

- The Bridge (*Die Brücke*) started in Dresden in 1905. The leaders of this group of artists were Ernst Ludwig Kirchner and Erich Heckel. Later, Emil Nolde joined the group. They mainly painted city scenes, portraits and human figures.

- The Blue Rider (*Der Blaue Reiter*) started in Munich in 1911. The founders were Wassily Kandinsky and Franz Marc. Other painters in the group were August Macke and Paul Klee.

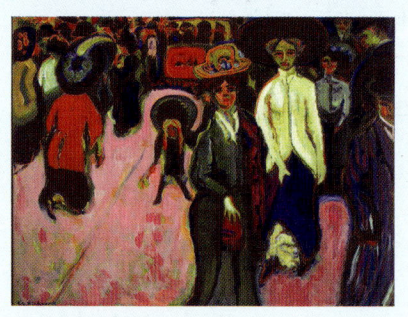

Ernst Ludwig Kirchner (Germany 1880 – Switzerland 1938)
Street, Dresden, 1908. Oil on canvas
Museum of Modern Art, New York

Paul Klee (Switzerland 1879 – Switzerland 1940)
Houses by the Sea, 1920. Watercolour on paper on cardboard
Private owner, Switzerland

▼ Cubism

Cubism was an art movement that completely changed European paintings. It started in France in 1907. Pablo Picasso, Georges Braque and Juan Gris were famous Cubist painters of that time. Cubist artists did not try to express their feelings and emotions. They experimented with structure. Cubists used geometrical forms like the cylinder, sphere and cone to represent the natural world. There were three main phases of Cubism:

- Early Cubism (1907–1909):
  The painters used bright colours.

- Analytical Cubism (1910–1912):
  The painters used monochromatic earth colours. They showed things as the mind, not the eyes, saw them.

- Synthetic Cubism (1912–1914):
  The painters introduced collaged objects into their paintings and the colours were brighter. Pablo Picasso and Georges Braque started to use pieces of cut-up newspaper in their paintings.

Pablo Picasso (Spain 1881 – France 1973)
Bread and Fruit Dish on a Table, 1909. Oil on canvas
Kunstmuseum, Basel

2 Play a guessing game

The painter was born in …
It's a/an … painting.
You can see it at …
Who painted it?
Which painting is it?

Super Tour 2

1 Say a painter's name and see if your classmates can find the correct art movement.
2 Make a timeline of art movements. Add the key dates from the text.
3 Present your work to the class or to a classmate.

2 Language stop

1 🔊 1.21 Listen, read and answer

Last Saturday I **went** on an art excursion with my youth club. There **were** three groups of young teenagers. I **was** in group one. Sarah, my sister, **was** in group one, too. Mark, my school friend, **was** in group two and my youth club friends, Andy and Marie, **were** in group three. An art teacher and three youth club leaders **accompanied** us.
We **met** at the train station at eight in the morning. We **got** on the train at eight thirty and we **arrived** in a small village at nine thirty. It **was** a slow train. Then we **walked** to a lake. There we **started** drawing. Some of the children **drew** the lake, others the trees or the flowers. At midday we **had** a packed lunch by the lake. After lunch, the art teacher **looked** at our drawings and **talked** about them. At five we **returned** to the train station and **travelled** back home. When we **arrived** home in the evening, I **was** very tired. On Sunday I **got** up very late!

> 1 Is the story about the present or the past? How do you know?
> 2 Look at the words in blue. What kind of words are they?
> 3 Is there a pattern?

2 🔊 1.22 Listen, repeat and answer

started	returned	walked
visited	arrived	talked
decorated	travelled	liked
wanted	played	finished

> 1 Look at these words. What is the same about all of them?
> 2 Listen to the words. Can you find a pattern in the green words, the red words and the blue words?

3 Read and answer

I went on an art excursion **on** Saturday.
We met at the train station at eight **in** the morning.
We got on the train **at** eight thirty.
At midday we had a packed lunch.
When we arrived home **in** the evening …
On Sunday I got up late.

> 1 Do you remember when we use *at*, *in* and *on*?

🎯 Super Tour 3

1 Write about an excursion you went on last week/month/year.
2 Tell a classmate about an excursion you went on last week/month/year.

Do you know that ...?

1 🔊 1.23 Listen and read

1 *Mona Lisa* is the most famous and probably the most valuable painting in the world. The original name of the painting was *Monna Lisa*. Monna is the short form for Madonna and means *My Lady* in Italian. So *Mona* was probably just a spelling mistake. Leonardo da Vinci (Italy 1452 – France 1519) painted *Mona Lisa* between 1503 and 1506. Leonardo loved the portrait and he always carried it with him. Now the painting is in the *Louvre* Museum in Paris and it belongs to the French government. About six million people visit the *Louvre* every year and most of them go to see *Mona Lisa*.

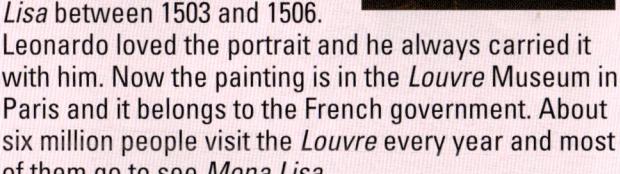

2 Vincent van Gogh (The Netherlands 1853 – France 1890) is one of the greatest modern European painters. He produced about 900 paintings and more than 1,000 drawings in a period of ten years, but he sold only one painting in his lifetime. Van Gogh became famous after his death. Here is one of van Gogh's paintings, *Vase with Fifteen Sunflowers*. He finished it in 1888. He painted several versions of the painting and one of them sold in 1987 for millions of dollars. There is a Vincent van Gogh museum in Amsterdam.

3  The State Hermitage Museum is the largest art gallery in the world. It is in Saint Petersburg in Russia. The museum was at one time the winter palace of the Tsars of Russia. The main part of the museum is in the winter palace, but it also includes five other buildings. Catherine the Great founded the museum in 1764 and it opened to the public in 1852. The museum has 322 galleries and hundreds and thousands of works of art.

4 Pablo Picasso (Spain 1881 – France 1973) is one of the world's most famous and most prolific painters. He constantly experimented with new art styles. Picasso created more than 13,000 paintings, 34,000 book illustrations and 300 sculptures and ceramics. His paintings are in the most important museums of the world as well as in private collections. There is a Picasso museum in Barcelona. Other Picasso museums are in Paris and Malaga.

Super Tour 4

1. On a map of Europe, mark and write the names of the cities where the museums in the texts are.
2. Choose one of the museums in the texts that you would like to visit. Tell a classmate and give reasons why.
3. Choose one of the museums in the texts that you would like to visit and write a short text about it. Use text 3 above and the Internet to help you.

2 Speak about a painting

Leonardo da Vinci painted this picture in ...

2 SKILLS TICKET

1 🔊 1.24 **Read**

Henri Matisse: A painting legend

1 Henri Matisse (France 1869 – France 1954) was one of the most famous artists of the 20th century. He was one of the leaders of the modern art movement. One of the main features of Matisse's work was the expressive use of colour. He used bold, bright colours together in a way that was surprising for people of the time.

2 His style changed completely over the years. His last works were mainly paper-cut paintings. He cut out pieces of paper and arranged them into shapes or images. Then he pasted them into position and painted them. One of these works was *Le Bateau (The Boat)*, finished in 1953.

3 In 1961, in the exhibition *The Last Works of Henri Matisse*, the Museum of Modern Art in New York hung the cut-out painting *Le Bateau* upside down and it remained upside down for 47 days. A visitor, who was a big fan of Matisse's paintings, noticed the mistake. She informed an attendant in the museum. Later she called a newspaper, *The New York Times*.

4 The newspaper published an article about the mistake and notified the director of the museum. The director immediately ordered museum staff to hang the painting properly.

5 *Le Bateau* shows the sail of the boat and its reflection in water. The lady visitor to the exhibition felt that the artist would never put the main motif (the sail) at the bottom and the less important motif (its reflection) on the top.

2 Read and answer

1 Who painted *Le Bateau*?
2 What technique did the painter use?
3 What mistake did the museum make?
4 Who noticed it?
5 What did this person do?
6 Who informed the director of the museum?

3 Ancient Egypt

In this unit you will
- learn about ancient Egyptian civilization and discover important facts about ancient Egyptians
- compare things
- use this knowledge to do a quiz

1 🎧 1.25 Listen and read

Egypt is in North Africa. Ancient Egyptian civilization started about 5000 years BC and it was very important for about 3,000 years. That is longer than other very important civilizations in history, for example, the Greek or the Roman civilizations. The ancient Egyptians lived on the banks of the River Nile, but their civilization ended over 2,000 years ago.

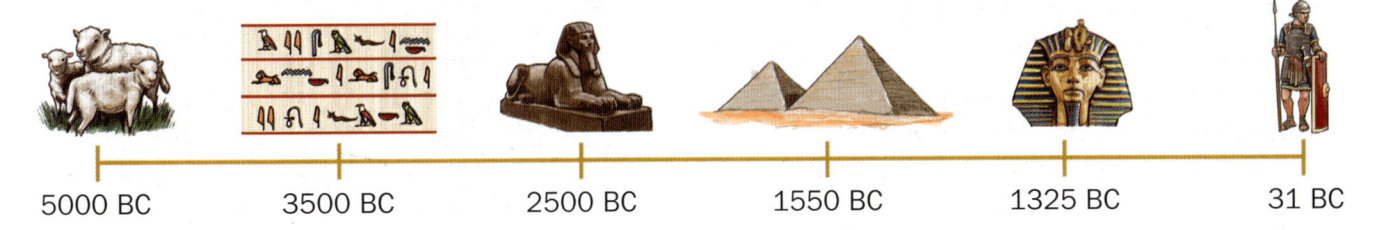

5000 BC — 3500 BC — 2500 BC — 1550 BC — 1325 BC — 31 BC

2 🎧 1.26 Read, listen and speak

How much do you know about ancient Egyptian civilization?

1. Why was the River Nile so important in ancient Egypt?
2. Was the pharaoh a man or a woman?
3. How many gods and goddesses were there in ancient Egypt?
4. What is a mummy?
5. Who was Cleopatra?
6. What is a scribe?
7. Why did the Egyptians build pyramids?
8. Who was Tutankhamun?
9. What is the Rosetta Stone?
10. What games did Egyptian children play?

pyramid — Cleopatra — a scribe — Tutankhamun — Thoth, the god of knowledge

Score
9-10 answers: You are an expert! Please share your knowledge with your classmates.
7-8 answers: Very good. You are almost an expert!
5-6 answers: Good. You already know a lot!
1-4 answers: A good start. Ancient Egyptian civilization is really interesting. Get ready to learn more!

Super Tour 1
What else do you want to know about ancient Egypt? Tell your classmates. Think about daily life, pharaohs, pyramids, writing, etc.

3 Story

Pharaoh Hatshepsut

3 🔴 1.27 **Look, listen and read**

When Pharaoh Thutmose II died, his wife, Hatshepsut, could not be the new pharaoh because she was a woman, not a man – but she declared herself Pharaoh Hatshepsut.

1

"The god Amun talked to me. Amun said, 'You are the new pharaoh.' So now I am Pharaoh Hatshepsut."

"Oh, no! She can't be the pharaoh! She's not a man! Only a man can be a pharaoh!"

"That's right! A female can't be a pharaoh!"

"She can't rule Egypt!"

2 But the high priest of Egypt and many other important people supported Hatshepsut.

"Yes, you are the pharaoh! We support you."

"Yes, you are the ruler of Egypt!"

"Long live the pharaoh!"

3 Now Hatshepsut was the 5th pharaoh of the 18th dynasty. It was the year 1479 BC. Hatshepsut decided to be called king, like a man, because many Egyptians did not want a woman to rule the country.

"I am the pharaoh. I am the king, not the queen! You must address me as a man."

4 The pharaoh had a lot of power and she also followed routines to make herself even more powerful and spectacular. Every day she got up very early.

"It's very early but it's time to get up. I have a long day ahead!"

26

Unit 3

5. Immediately lots of servants came to Hatshepsut. First, she had a bath. Then her servants put lots of perfume on her body and make-up on her face. In Egypt, perfume and make-up were very important for men and for women. They were also very important for the pharaoh.

"This new perfume is really good."

"This new make-up is excellent."

Sometimes Hatshepsut put on a false beard, a symbol of power.

"This beard gives you pharaonic power."

6. Then she got dressed. She dressed like a male pharaoh. She put on bracelets and necklaces as a sign of power.

"Do you like your new clothes, His Majesty?"

"Look at these new bracelets and necklaces. Do you like them?"

"Yes, I like the new clothes and the jewels, too."

7. When she was ready, she began work. She worked very hard. Every day she met different people in the audience chamber: ambassadors from other countries, military leaders and important people in Egypt.

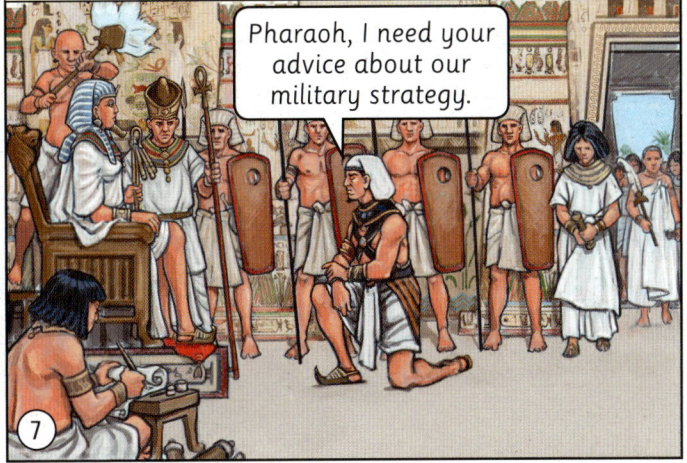

"Pharaoh, I need your advice about our military strategy."

8. Then Pharaoh Hatshepsut went to the temple to honour the god Amun. She was a divine majesty, but Amun was the king of the gods. Hatshepsut asked Amun questions. The high priest answered her questions on behalf of Amun. Then they offered a sacrifice to the gods.

"Amun, what's good for Egypt?"

"Amun said, 'Keep society in good order and start trading with more countries.'"

9. Sometimes, the pharaoh visited the sites of the many important new buildings and monuments in Egypt. She decided to build a great temple at Deir el Bahari.

"When I die, I want to be buried here."

3 Story

10 Hatshepsut also visited the farmers and traders by the River Nile.

"Pharaoh, our crops are good. We have lots of corn and barley."

"And we have lots of flax. We can make lots of good linen with it."

11 Hatshepsut ruled Egypt for about 20 years. During that time the economy in Egypt was really good. Commerce and trading with other countries was excellent. There were no big wars. The Egyptians built very important buildings.

12 But one day …

"Who's that man?"

"I don't know."

"What does he want?"

"I don't know. Let's see!"

13 "Listen! I am Thutmose III. I am the son of Pharaoh Thutmose II. I was very young when my father died. I am a man so it was my place to be the pharaoh, but Hatshepsut wanted to rule Egypt all by herself. Now Hatshepsut can't continue to be the pharaoh. I am the pharaoh. I am the ruler of Egypt!"

14 Hatshepsut disappeared and we do not know what happened to her. But we know that she was a great pharaoh.

4 Read and answer

Hatshepsut was a woman pharaoh. She lived in Egypt around 3,500 years ago. She built many important buildings. One of them was the temple of Deir el Bahari.

1 Who was Hatshepsut?
2 Where did she live?
3 When did she live?
4 Did she build any temples?

Temple of Deir el Bahari

5 Tell the story

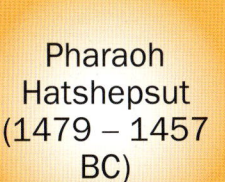

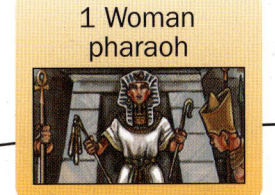

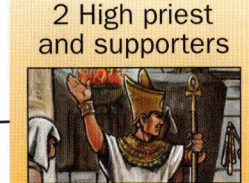

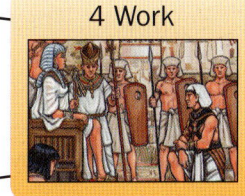

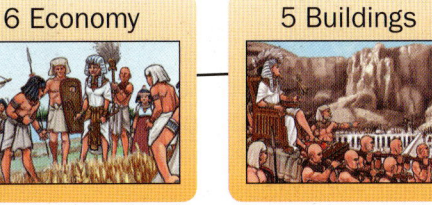

Pharaoh Hatshepsut (1479 – 1457 BC)

1 Woman pharaoh
2 High priest and supporters
3 Daily life
4 Work
5 Buildings
6 Economy
7 Successor

Super Tour 2

Write the story in your own words.

6 Play a team game

Four thousand, eight hundred and fifty

Team A	Team B
1,200	2,400
3,500	3,999
1,479	4,850
5,000	5,000
4,850	1,479
3,999	3,500
2,400	1,200

3 About ancient Egypt

1 🔊 1.29 **Listen and read**

The River Nile
The River Nile (6,695 kilometres) is the longest river in the world. The banks of the river are very fertile. Beyond the banks of the river is the desert: no water! Ancient Egyptians lived and farmed on the banks of the River Nile. The River Nile made ancient Egypt a great, rich civilization. Every year between June and October the river flooded because the snow in the far away mountains melted in summer. Then the river banks were under water. The country was like a sea. When the water disappeared, the Egyptians planted their crops on the wet lands. Ancient Egyptians thought that the River Nile was a god, the god Hapy.

Farming by the Nile

2 🔊 1.30 **Listen and read**

Pyramids
The pyramids were the tombs of the pharaohs. The afterlife was very important for ancient Egyptians. They wanted to preserve the body for a long time so that the dead person could make a long journey to Heaven. That is the reason why they mummified the body and buried it in a pyramid.

Pyramids were the first buildings in history that were made with big blocks of stone. The stones were cut and put together with great precision. The Great Pyramid of Giza is 146 metres high. It has 2,300,000 blocks of stone. Each block weighs 2,500 kilograms. The Great Pyramid of Giza is the oldest and the largest pyramid in Giza.

The Sphinx is in front of all the pyramids in Giza. It has the body of a lion and the head of a pharaoh.

A mummified body (a mummy)

The Sphinx

The pyramids of Giza

3 🔊 1.32 Listen and read

Egyptian writing

The ancient Egyptians did not use letters to write, they used pictures. Each picture is a hieroglyph. Only rich boys went to school to learn to read and write. They had to learn more than 700 signs and how to combine them to communicate in writing.
A scribe was a person who could read and write. It was a very difficult job! Scribes used black or red ink and they wrote on papyrus (paper). Thanks to scribes, we know a lot about ancient Egypt.

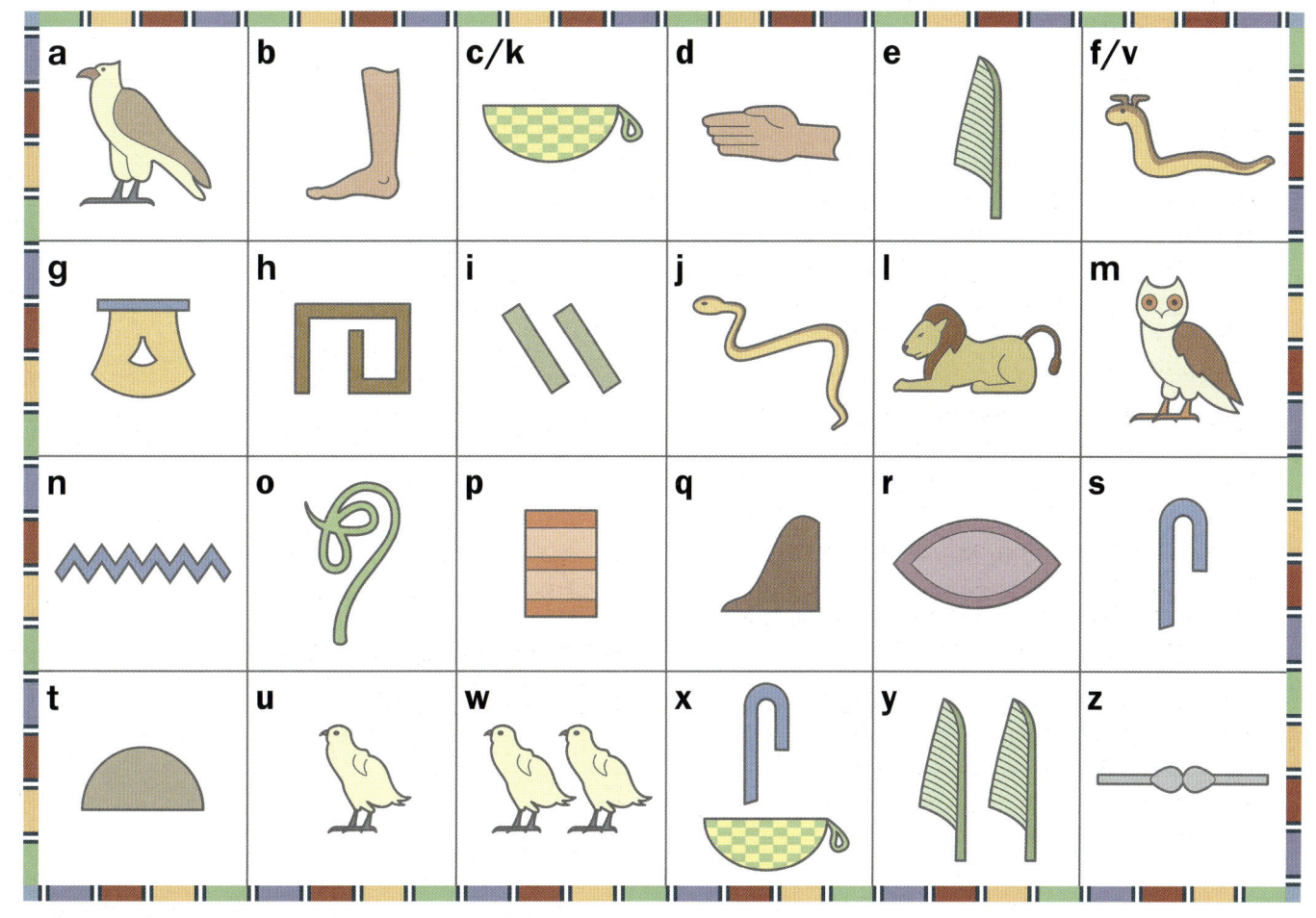

Super Tour 3

1 Write your name in hieroglyphs. Use the table to help you.
2 Write a message in hieroglyphs and give it to a classmate. Can they read it?
3 Make a poster about the pyramids of Giza. Include as much of the information from text 2 as possible.

3 Language stop

1 🔊 1.33 Compare

The River Mississippi: 6,275 km
The River Amazon: 6,400 km
The River Nile: 6,695 km

The River Mississippi is **long**.
The River Amazon is **longer than** the River Mississippi.
The River Nile is **the longest** river in the world.

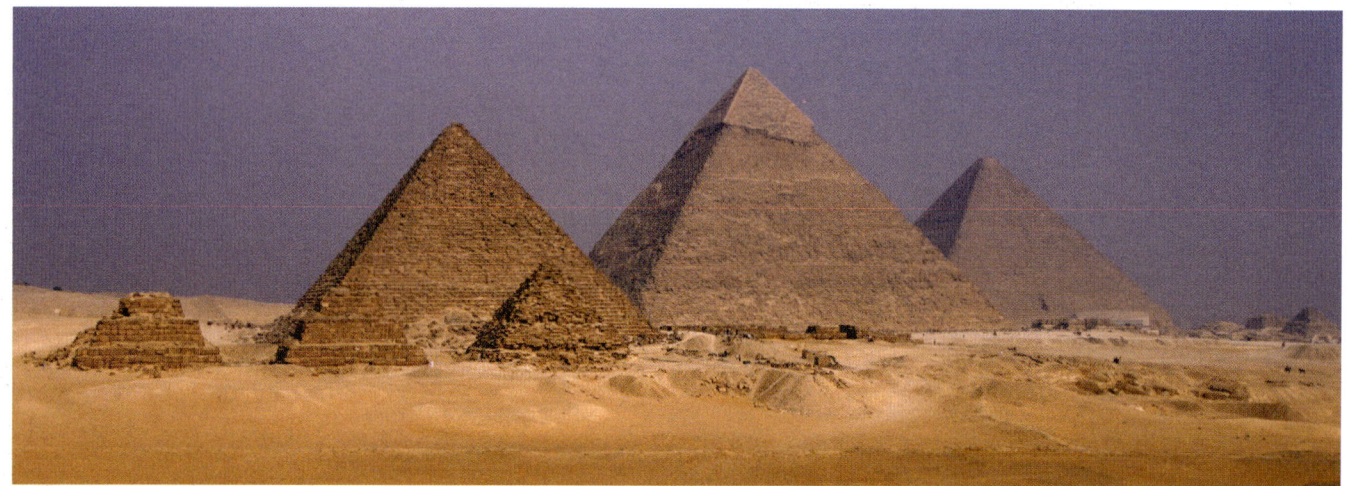

The three pyramids of Giza are really **old** and **large**.
The group of pyramids is **spectacular**.
The Great Pyramid is **older**, **larger** and **more spectacular than** the other two pyramids of Giza.
In fact, the Great Pyramid is **the oldest**, **the highest** and **the largest** of the three pyramids of Giza. It is also **the most spectacular** and **the most amazing** pyramid in the group.

> 1 Look at the words in **red**. What kind of words are these?
> 2 Can you find a pattern?
> 3 Make a rule.
> 4 Is there a rule in your language, too?

2 Find the answers

Why did Hatshepsut wear a false beard?   **Because** the snow melted in the faraway mountains.
Why did the River Nile flood?   **Because** they used them as tombs for the pharaohs.
Why did the Egyptians build pyramids?   **Because** it was a symbol of power.

> 1 Look at the words in **red**. Can you see the rule?
> 2 How do you say this in your language?

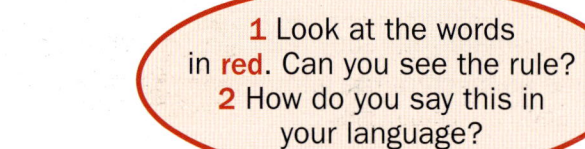

Do you know that ...?

1 🔊 1.34 **Listen and read**

1 Gods and goddesses
In ancient Egypt there were about 2,000 gods and goddesses. These are some examples:

Amun: King of the gods

Isis: Queen of the gods

Ra: The sun god

Sobek: God with a crocodile head. He controlled the waters. He was the guard of gods. Many gods had animal heads.

Anuke: Goddess of war

2 Games
Some Egyptian games were very similar to the games we play today. Board games were very popular and everybody played them: adults and children. Some examples of board games are: Senet, Snake, Dogs and Jackals. Egyptian children also played ball games and had toys made of clay or wood.

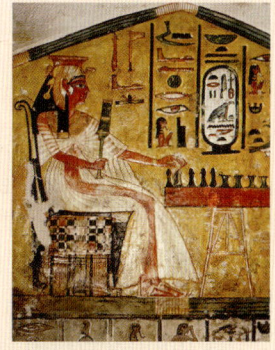

Woman playing a board game

3 Pets
Crocodiles were very special animals for ancient Egyptians. Rich people had crocodiles as pets. There were crocodiles in temples, too. The crocodiles lived in pools and were free to move around because they were not in cages. Can you imagine the danger? Sometimes the crocodiles had jewels: bracelets, necklaces and rings!

4 Cleopatra
Cleopatra was the last pharaoh of Egypt. She was only 15 years old when she became a pharaoh. The Roman leader Julius Caesar helped her to win a battle and keep the Egyptian throne. Cleopatra went to Rome with Caesar, but when Caesar died, Cleopatra returned to Egypt and asked the Roman Marc Antony to help her. He tried to help her, but she lost the Egyptian throne in 31 BC.

5 The Rosetta Stone
The Rosetta Stone has writing inscribed on it. The text is in three languages: Hieroglyphic, Demotic and Greek. The text was written in 196 BC but the stone was discovered in 1799 by the French. Thanks to the Rosetta Stone we now know a lot about ancient Egyptian civilization. It helped scholars to understand Egyptian hieroglyphs.

3 SKILLS TICKET

1 🔊 1.35 Read

The discovery of Tutankhamun's tomb

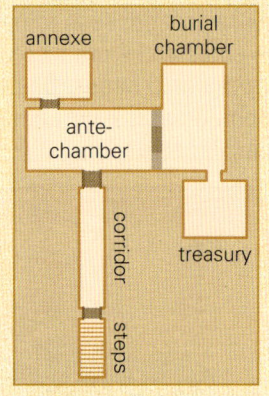

(diagram labels: annexe, burial chamber, antechamber, corridor, treasury, steps)

Tutankhamun was born in 1341 BC. His father was Pharaoh Akehenhaten, who died when Tutankhamun was nine years old. Tutankhamun died at the age of 18, but we know a lot about him because a British archaeologist, Howard Carter, found his tomb. This is the story of the discovery:

Howard Carter: *Lord Carnarvon, please listen to me. I have lots of documents and I think that Tutankhamun's tomb is in the Valley of the Kings, where many other pharaohs were buried. I want to find that tomb. But I need money to excavate and find the tomb.*
Lord Carnarvon: *OK. You can have the money.*

But after five years of work, Howard Carter did not find the tomb. Lord Carnarvon was very disappointed. He did not want to pay more money. But Carter convinced him once again.

Howard Carter: *Just one more year, please. I will find the tomb.*
Lord Carnarvon: *Well … I don't know … all right. But only one more year.*

Carter continued working in the Valley of the Kings and, on the morning of 4th November 1922, one of his workers noticed a very strange rock. It was a step of a staircase! They excavated a little more and found a door. Carter knew immediately that it was an important finding because the door was sealed and it had the stamp of royal tombs.

Carter did not open the door. He sent a telegram to Lord Carnarvon in England.

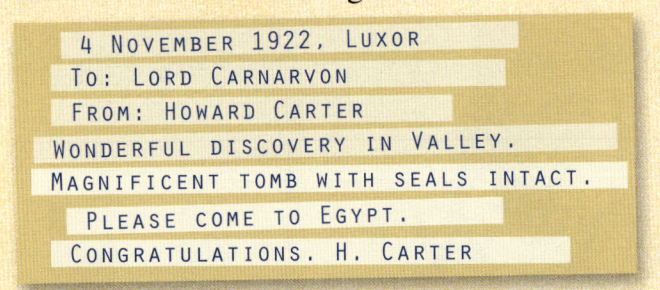

```
4 November 1922, Luxor
To: Lord Carnarvon
From: Howard Carter
Wonderful discovery in Valley.
Magnificent tomb with seals intact.
Please come to Egypt.
Congratulations. H. Carter
```

Lord Carnarvon and his daughter arrived in Egypt on 23rd November 1922. On Saturday, 25th November, Carter removed the sealed door. He noticed that he was not the first person to visit the tomb. Robbers had tried to enter and steal the treasure. But Carter found a second door. He opened a tiny hole and looked through it. At first he could not see anything because it was completely dark. But after a little while he could distinguish strange animals, statues of gold and many more golden objects.

At last Carter entered the different rooms in the tomb, over 3,000 years after the pharaoh died. Everything was in perfect condition. There were even flowers with petals.

Tutankhamun's tomb was very small compared to the tombs of other pharaohs in Egypt, but Carter found over 3,000 objects plus the pharaoh's mummy. Thanks to this discovery we know about Pharaoh Tutankhamun and about life in ancient Egypt.

2 Read and answer

1 When did Tutankhamun die?
2 How many years was Tutankhamun the pharaoh?
3 Who was Howard Carter?
4 Who was Lord Carnarvon?
5 What happened on 4th November 1922?

4 Water on Earth

In this unit you will
- learn about the importance of water in everyday life and problems with water
- ask questions and give short answers in the present simple and past simple and use adverbs of frequency
- use this knowledge to plan, write and present part of a project on water

1 🔊 2.01 Listen and find

Sebastian Foster
Class 6 BD
March 20 ____

My project on water

Contents

1 Introduction to water

2 Where water comes from

3 Water in farming and other industries

4 Water and people

5 Water in the developing world

6 Water and the weather: droughts, floods and other problems

7 Water energy and water conservation

8 Conclusion

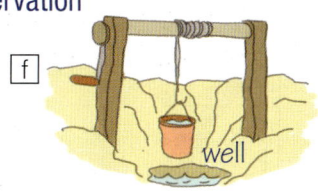

2 🔊 2.02 Listen and read

Introduction to water
Water covers most of the Earth's surface. 97% of the Earth's water is in the oceans, but it is salty and not good for people to use. 2.3% of the Earth's water is frozen in glaciers and polar ice caps. This frozen water is the largest reservoir of freshwater. 0.5% is groundwater – water running underground. 0.2% is in rivers and lakes. Most of the water we use at home comes from rivers and lakes. Only 0.001% is in the air as water vapour.
Water is essential for life. Every human, plant and animal needs water to live. Industries need water, too. The farming industry uses around 70% of the world's freshwater and other industries use around 20%. The rest is for domestic use – we use it at home to eat, drink, wash, etc.
The increase of the world's population and changes to the climate are affecting the quantity and quality of freshwater available on Earth. Sometimes there is too much water, sometimes there is not enough, and sometimes it is not safe to drink. Over 1.1 billion people do not have clean drinking water.
Without water, there would be no life on Earth. Don't waste it!

4 Story

A visit to a water project

3 🔊 2.04 **Look, listen and read**

1. Hi! My name's Sophie and this is my brother Josh. We live in London with our mum and dad. Mum works for an organization called WaterAid. It supports projects in countries where people don't have access to clean drinking water. Here, we can turn on a tap to get the clean water we need. But in many other parts of the world, people don't have a supply of safe water. Last year, Mum took us to visit a WaterAid project in Malawi, a country in southern Africa.

2. We went into the countryside to visit small villages with the coordinator of the project. His name was Bomani. He showed us the wells where people go to collect water. They were a long way from the villages.

— The water is very dirty.
— Yes, but people come here to collect it because there is nothing better. They often get ill from drinking this water.

3. Bomani talked to a woman at the well and translated for us.

— Do you come here every day?
— Yes, she does. It usually takes five hours to walk here and back to the village with buckets full of water.
— Five hours!

4. We went to other villages where the situation was very different.

— There's a well in the village … and the water is clean! Did WaterAid build it?
— No, we didn't.

5. The regional government built this well. It started a programme to build wells in all the villages in the region, but then it ran out of money. Now some villages have wells and some don't.

36

Unit 4

6. But we don't know where the wells are because there are no records.

7. And that's a problem because you need to know where there are wells already. Then you can plan to build new ones in the right places.

That's right, Josh. In fact, that's what we're working on at the moment. We're creating a record of the wells.

8. It's called mapping water. When we have a map of all the wells in the region, we can see where people need new ones. Let's add this well to the record.

Do you mark it on a map?

9. No, we don't. Many of these villages are too small to appear on a map. We use a GPS satellite positioning system. The information goes to a central database and we can create a map of all the wells in the region very quickly.

Great!

10. We visited more villages to map water. We were sorry when it was time to leave.

Thanks for everything, Bomani. The map is almost complete. What happens next?

I go to the villages where we are going to build new wells. We discuss what we can all contribute to the building process. Why don't you come back next year and see how we get on?

4 Story

11. We were lucky. We returned to Malawi this summer to visit the project again. Bomani took us to see one of the new wells.

"It's fantastic! But I'm a bit surprised. Why is it only made of rope and a wheel? There are better ways of building wells."

12. "That's true, but we always use materials that the people in the village can find easily. They need to maintain the wells themselves. So we build simple wells and the repairs cost nothing."

13. "Hello. We met at the old well last year. Do you remember us?"

"Yes, I do."

14. "Do you have problems collecting water now?"

"No, I don't. I never spend five hours going to the well now. It usually takes ten minutes. The water is clean and people don't get ill."

15. "We have time to work in our gardens. We can grow more food for our families. We often take vegetables to sell at the market. The money we earn helps us provide for our children. Life is better."

16. Josh and I learnt a lot from our trip to Malawi. We saw what organizations like WaterAid do and why. Most of all, we saw for ourselves how important it is to have access to clean water.

Unit 4

4 Which words belong to which picture? Speak

countryside · ill · GPS satellite · dirty · central database · other villages · map water · regional government · record · new well · buckets · maintain · coordinator · rope · wheel · well · clean · material · five hours · programme · repairs · ran out of money · one year later

5 Use the words and pictures to summarize the story

This story is about a water project ...   One year later ...

6 Speak

This photograph shows ...   I think it's interesting that ...

Super Tour 1

1 Think about what happened in the villages when Sophie and Josh left. And what do you think happened to Sophie and Josh? Did they go back to Malawi? Talk to your classmates.

2 Find out the names and locations of other projects which help people get access to clean drinking water in other countries around the world. Use the Internet and books.

39

4 About water on Earth

1 🔊 2.05 **Listen and read**

The water cycle

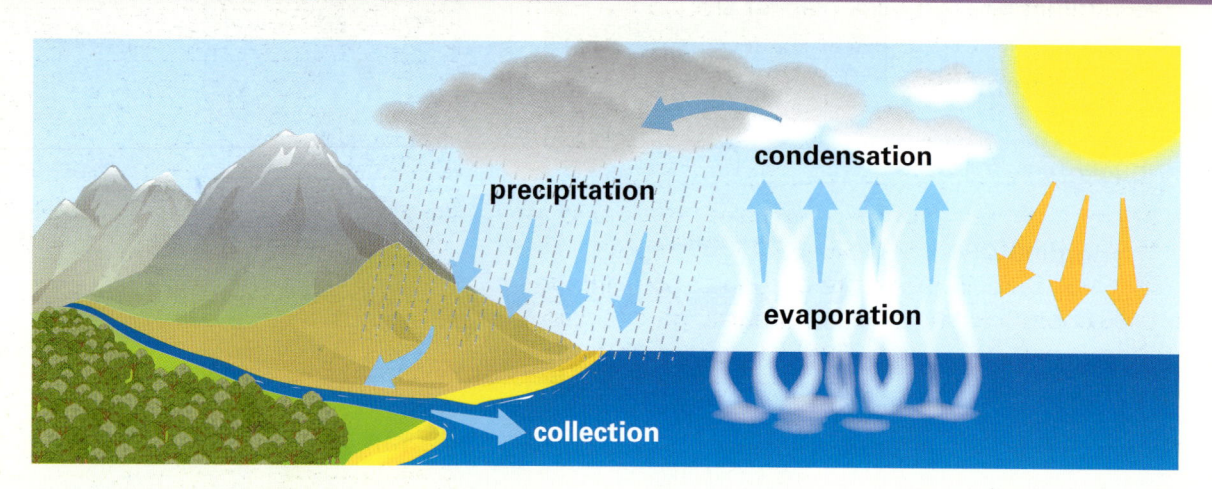

Our planet recycles water in a continuous movement we know as the water cycle. This is the journey that water takes as it circulates from the Earth to the sky and back to the Earth again, and this journey never ends.

- First the sun heats water in the oceans, rivers and lakes, and changes this water into a gas called water vapour. This is **evaporation**.
- Water vapour is a very light gas which rises into the sky. There the air is colder and the water vapour cools and forms very small drops of liquid water that become clouds. This is **condensation**.
- The wind moves the clouds and the drops join together. They get big and heavy, and the drops fall from the clouds as rain, sleet, snow or hail. This water that falls from the sky is **precipitation**.
- The water falls on the land. Then the oceans, rivers and lakes 'collect' it. This is **collection**. And from here, the journey of water starts once more.

2 Speak

What do you call it when water changes into a gas called water vapour?

That's evaporation. OK, what do you call it when …

3 🔊 2.06 Read and listen

Why is the Earth getting warmer?

The atmosphere is a thick blanket around the Earth. The sun heats the Earth and natural greenhouse gases – water vapour, ozone, carbon dioxide – in tiny amounts in the atmosphere keep the Earth and everything on it warm. We know this as the greenhouse effect. Industries burn fossil fuels – coal, oil and natural gases – to make plastic and other products and to make electricity in power stations. This releases more carbon dioxide into the atmosphere. Cutting down and burning trees also releases carbon dioxide. But too much of this gas means that the atmosphere becomes thicker and the Earth gets warmer. That's the cause of global warming – the increase in the temperature of the Earth's atmosphere.

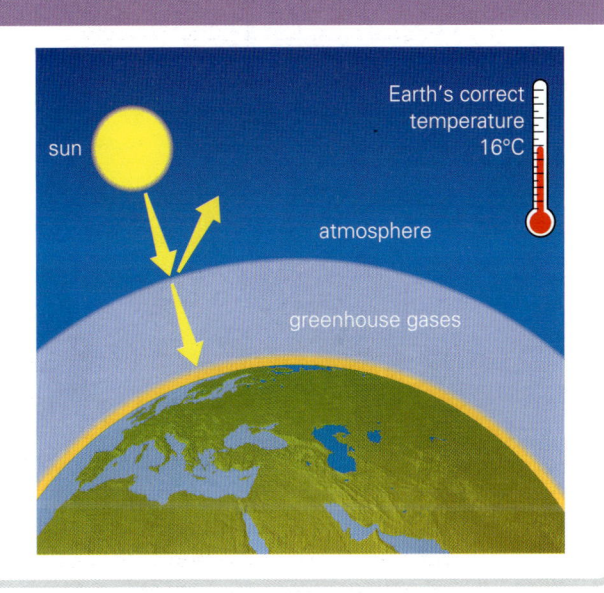

4 🔊 2.07 Listen and read

How does global warming affect us?

Glaciers form in places with heavy snowfall in winter. Continental glaciers, or ice caps, cover large areas of land in the polar regions of the Arctic and the Antarctic. Alpine glaciers are in high mountain valleys around the world. Global warming is causing glaciers to melt. Switzerland is the home of the largest alpine glacier in Europe, but 12% of Swiss glaciers melted in the past ten years. When glaciers melt, the water flows into the oceans, rivers and lakes. If this continues, sea levels will rise and some islands and coastal towns and cities will disappear under water. Floods and storms will be more frequent and more severe in parts of the world.

In other parts of the world, it will be much hotter with less precipitation, so rivers and lakes will dry up. Deserts will be larger and there will be more droughts.

Super Tour 2

1. Do you think there was more snow or rain last winter than the previous winter in your country? Talk to your classmates.
2. Make a list of the biggest glaciers in your country, or choose a country with glaciers. Do you think they are melting? Find out on the Internet.

4 Language stop

1 🔊 2.08 Listen, look and find three mistakes

Name	turn off tap	last night / this morning	have a short shower
Victor	✓		
Eva	✓		
Robin	✓		
George	✓		
Karen	✓		
Mr Norman	✓		
Carla	✓	✗	
Ben	✓	✓	
Lucy	✗	✗	
Charlie	✗	✗	
Simon	✓		

2 Read and answer

Victor **Do** you usually turn off the tap when you clean your teeth?
Mr Norman Of course I **do**. And what about you, Victor?
Victor Yes, I **do**. Eva **does**. And Robin and George **do**.
Ben But I **don't**. Simon **doesn't** … and Lucy and Charlie **don't**.
Mr Norman **Did** you turn off the tap last night, Ben?
Ben Yes, I **did**, but Lucy and Charlie **didn't**.

> 1 Look at the words in blue. When do we use *do* or *does* in answers? And *don't* or *doesn't*?
> 2 When do we use *did* or *didn't*?
> 3 How do we make questions in the present simple and past simple?

3 Read and answer

Mr Norman I **always** turn off the tap.
Victor Do you **usually** turn off the tap?
Simon I **never** turn it off.

> 1 Look at the words in red. What do they mean?
> 2 Do they go before or after the main verb?

4 Make true sentences

	always	have a short shower.
	usually	water the plants with rain water.
I	often	water the plants with washing-up water.
	sometimes	turn off the tap when I clean my teeth.
	never	use a bucket to wash the car.

Super Tour 3

When do you waste water and when do you save water? Write a text using *always*, *usually*, *often*, *sometimes* and *never*.

Do you know that ...?

1 🎧 2.09 **Listen and choose**

- Water and the weather: droughts, floods and other problems
- Water energy and water conservation
- Water in farming and other industries
- Water in the developing world
- Water and people

2 🎧 2.09 **Listen and read**

1 In the developed world, a person uses an average of 150 litres of water a day for drinking, cleaning, washing and cooking. In the developing world, people who have access to a water source such as a well within one kilometre, but not in their house or garden, use between 10 and 20 litres a day.

2 75% of a baby's body weight is water. As the baby grows up, this changes to around 60% for men and 55% for women. Water helps us to stay healthy, and there is water in all of our organs. It keeps the body cool and keeps our blood thin. It also breaks down food. But our body loses water all the time. That's why it's important to drink a lot of water because our body can't work without it.

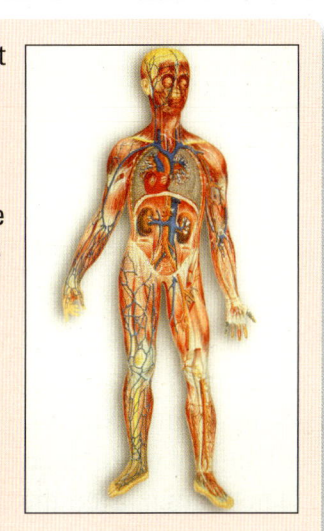

3 Water is one of the oldest sources of energy. It's also one of the cleanest and cheapest sources. The Greek word *hydro* means water, and hydropower is the energy that comes from the force of moving water. Ancient Greeks and Romans used water wheels to grind grain into flour. Today hydroelectric power plants use the energy of water falling from high dams – barriers built across rivers – to make electricity. The first hydroelectric power plant in the world was built in the late 19th century at Niagara Falls, on the border of Canada and the USA.

4 When power stations, factories, cars and lorries burn fossil fuels, they produce acid gases. Most of these gases go up very high into the atmosphere and mix with the clouds. When precipitation happens, the rain is acidic. Acid rain damages forests, lakes and rivers. Trees lose their leaves and can die, plants don't grow properly and fish and the birds that eat them can die, too.

5 Rain is the easiest way to water plants and crops in farmers' fields, but when there isn't enough rain, people use irrigation. This is an artificial way of watering plants and crops. There are different kinds of irrigation. Sprinklers spray water at high pressure over fields of crops. Sub-irrigation is when water comes from a system of pipes below the plants to give them the drink they need to live. This system is common in greenhouses. Today, because we need to conserve water, modern irrigation means plants get just the right amount of water they need.

6 The koala bear is one of the few animals that don't drink water. Koalas live in the eucalyptus forests of eastern and south-eastern Australia. They eat a lot of eucalyptus leaves to get the water they need.

Super Tour 4

1 Write down how many times you use water each day and what you use it for.
2 Do you think you use more or less than 150 litres of water a day? Talk to your classmates.

4 SKILLS TICKET

1 🎯 2.10 Read

The race to the South Pole

1 The South Pole is on the continent of Antarctica. Antarctica is the coldest and driest continent on Earth, with a minimum temperature of -80ºC in winter. Ice caps cover 98% of the continent, which is also home to 70% of the world's freshwater. There are no permanent residents, only around 1,000 people working at the research stations there.

2 In 1910, British Captain Robert Scott and Norwegian explorer Roald Amundsen planned expeditions to reach the South Pole. Captain Robert Scott wanted to study emperor penguins and place the British flag at the South Pole. Amundsen said that he wanted to study the Southern Sea, but he really wanted to be the first to reach the South Pole.

3 Scott departed on his ship, the *Terra Nova*, from Cardiff, Wales, with three motor sledges, 19 ponies, 33 dogs and 24 men in June 1910. Amundsen left Oslo on the ship *Fram* in August 1910 with nearly a 100 sledge dogs, sledges and 19 men.

4 In January 1911, Amundsen reached Antarctica and set up a base camp. The Norwegian team built a small wooden hut and they spent the first months there organizing depots of food and equipment southward and making preparations for the long journey to the South Pole.

5 Amundsen's final journey began in October 1911 with five men on sledges pulled by dogs. They finally reached the South Pole on 14th December 1911. They set up a camp and stayed there for three days checking that they really were at the South Pole. Then they planted the Norwegian flag there and started the journey back to their base camp as winners of the race.

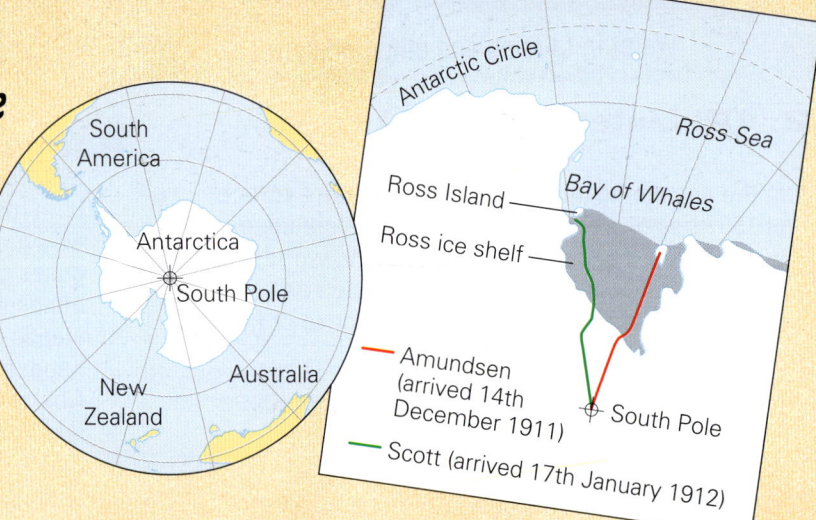

6 Scott's team also arrived in Antarctica in January 1911 and set up their base camp. Scott planned to organize different depots using his motor sledges, but they broke down. The team started the race to the South Pole in November 1911 using the ponies to transport food and equipment, but the ponies started sinking into the soft snow and some died.

7 Scott chose four members of his team to go with him on the final stage of the journey to the South Pole. The five men were pulling the sledges themselves when they reached the South Pole, exhausted, on 17th January 1912 and found the Norwegian flag already flying there.

2 Read and answer

1 Where is the South Pole?
2 What did Captain Scott want to study?
3 Who used ponies in the expedition?
4 What happened on 14th December 1911?
5 What did Scott find when he reached the South Pole?

5 Architecture

In this unit you will
- learn about architecture, interesting buildings and materials
- use the simple future with *will* and *won't* and adverbs of sequence
- use this knowledge to plan, hold and write up an interview

1 🔊 2.11 Speak and listen

1 What is architecture? Is it an art? Is it a science? What do you think?
2 What does an architect do? What does an engineer do?
3 Do architects and engineers work together?

Architecture is an art and it is a science, too: it is the art and the science of designing buildings. We can also speak about the architecture of a building. This means the style and materials of the construction. An architect is the person who designs buildings. An engineer is the person responsible for the technical part of the building's design.
Architects and engineers usually work together to build interesting solid buildings. The contractors or builders are the companies that do the building work.

2 🔊 2.12 Read, listen and speak

How much do you know about architecture?

solar panels

1 Can you name an important architect?
2 What is a skyscraper?
3 What is a green roof?
4 Can you name five building materials?
5 What stops heat escaping from a building: insulation or solar panels?
6 Where is the Empire State Building?
7 Where is the Rolex Learning Centre?
8 Who were the skywalkers?
9 Who designed the Tate Modern art gallery in London?
10 Where is the tallest building in the world?

skyscraper

a green roof

building materials

Score
9-10 answers: Excellent! You love architecture! Please share your knowledge with your classmates.
7-8 answers: Very good. You already know quite a lot!
5-6 answers: You are good. Get ready to learn a lot more!
1-4 answers: Architecture is really interesting. Join the class to learn a lot about it!

Super Tour 1

1 What interesting buildings do you know in your town or city? Tell your classmates.
2 Explain why you know about these buildings: Did you visit them? Did you read about them?
3 Which interesting buildings around the world would you like to visit? Tell your classmates.

5 Story

The Empire State Building

3 🔊 2.13 **Look, listen and read**

1. This was the city of New York in the 1920s. There were many tall buildings already, but rich people wanted to build taller buildings as a symbol of power. There was a race to build the tallest building in the city and in the world.

2. Late in 1929, John J. Raskob, a very important businessman, visited the offices of the architects Shreve, Lamb and Harmon Associates.

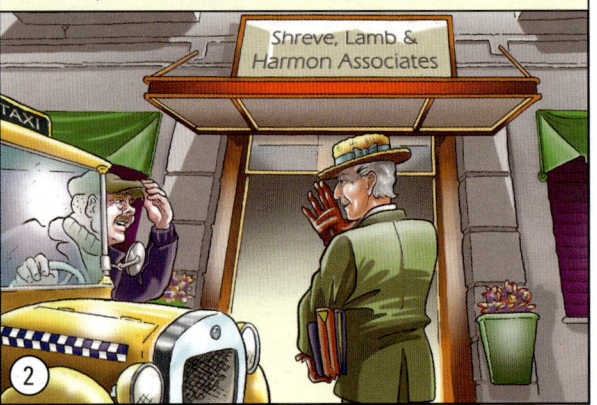

3. Raskob wanted to talk to architect William F. Lamb about a new project.

— I want to build the tallest skyscraper in New York. The Chrysler Building is going to be really tall when they finish it. That's why I want a taller one. And I want it immediately.

— Well, that will cost a lot of money.

— No problem. I have an excellent company of investors: the Empire State, Inc.

4. Within only a few days, Shreve, Lamb and Harmon Associates agreed to build a skyscraper taller than the Chrysler Building in a very short time.

— When will the building plans be ready? We don't want to waste a minute!

— They'll be ready in two weeks. We'll build 102 floors, it'll be the tallest building in the world and we'll finish in only 18 months. It'll cost $50 million, including the land.

5. Now the investors and the architects needed good contractors to build the skyscraper. General contractors Starrett Brothers and Eken, very important builders at that time, agreed to do the job on time.

— This project is extremely complex. The size and the characteristics of the new building will create unusual challenges. We won't use the building equipment that we have now because it isn't suitable for this project. We'll design and buy new specialized equipment.

— We'll develop a very solid structure and we'll build fast and provide the best quality.

6 Soon everyone involved in the planning of the project was very busy. If they did not work in total coordination or did not fulfil their responsibilities, things were not going to work well.

7 The excavation for the new building started in January 1930. Two groups of 300 men worked day and night. First, they created the foundations for the 210 columns needed to support the structure. This was not an easy task because there was solid rock under the ground.

8 Then, in March 1930, the builders started the steel skeleton of the building. They built about four and a half floors a week – an amazing speed! They used about 60,000 tons of steel.

9 To make the construction easier and more efficient, the contractors developed some innovations that saved time, money and effort. For example, to move the materials, they built a railway at the construction site. The railway cars were pushed by men, but the cars could hold a lot, so in the end they saved time and effort.

10 The workers earned $15 a day. That was a high salary in the 1930s.

— How many workers are there?

— We have 3,500 men working at the same time. They work every day, Sundays and holidays included.

47

5 Story

11. While some of the workers completed the outside of the skyscraper, others, such as electricians and plumbers, worked in the interior installing the essential facilities of the building.

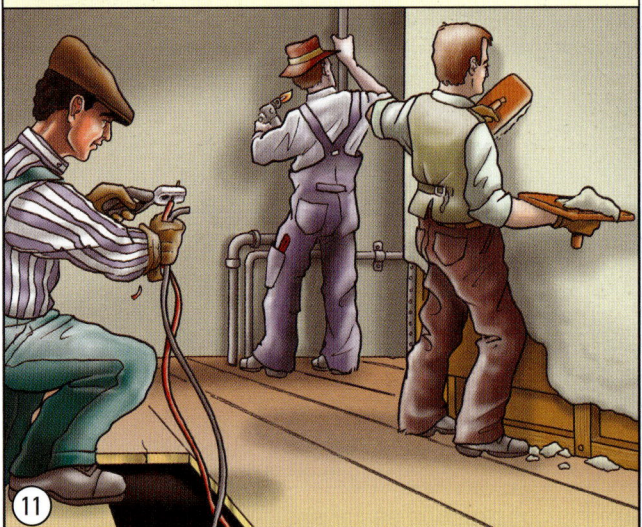

12. Apart from the 60,000 tons of steel, the contractors used ten million bricks, 47,400 cubic metres of concrete, around 1,000 square metres of marble, over 750 kilometres of electrical wire, 193 kilometres of pipe and 1,600 kilometres of telephone cable.

— So ... how many windows will there be?
— 6,500. And there'll be 1,860 steps, 73 lifts and 2,500 toilets.

The Empire State Building was completed in one year and 45 days and the total cost was around $41 million. This means that they finished the skyscraper before the agreed deadline and under the estimated cost.

13. *The Daily Clarion* — BUILT IN 410 DAYS FOR $41 MILLION — $9 M UNDER BUDGET

14. The skyscraper has 102 floors and it is 381 metres high.

— Our building is taller than the Chrysler Building! The Empire State Building is the tallest building in the world! We are the winners of the building race!

15. On 1st May 1931, the Empire State Building opened to the public. It was the tallest building in the world until the 1970s. Today it is still an architectural symbol on the skyline of New York City.

— People will remember this for years to come!

Unit 5

4 Tell the story

The Empire State Building (New York, 1930 – 1931)

1 Building race 
2 Architects 
3 Contractors 
4 Cooperating 
5 Building process 
6 Challenges 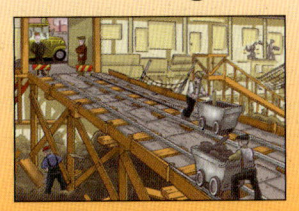
7 Workers and salary 
8 Materials 
9 The finished building

> **Super Tour 2**
>
> Look at the newspaper headline on page 48. Imagine you are a journalist and write the story to go with the headline.

5 Put the information in order and tell the story of the Chrysler Building

a. Built for: Walter P. Chrysler, owner of the Chrysler Car Corporation

b. Materials: 3,826,000 bricks, 29,961 tons of steel, 5,000 windows

c. The completed building: cost $20 million, completed on 28th May 1930, world's tallest building until Empire State Building - 319 metres, 77 floors, 32 lifts, red marble walls

d. Architect: William Van Alen, New York City

e. Building race: against Bank of Manhattan, four floors a week

f. Building process: top of building built inside, in secret, to win race

The Chrysler Building (New York, 1928 – 1930)

5 About architecture

1 🔊 2.16 **Listen and read**

Eco-buildings

When an architect designs an eco-building, he or she will take great care to use the right materials and to design systems that are environmentally friendly. This means that the building will be healthy for its occupants. It will also be healthy, or friendly, for the environment around it. For example, by using solar panels, the building will be able to create its own clean energy from the sun. This can provide hot water and central heating. Double or triple-glazed windows provide insulation. They help to keep the building warm in winter and stop heat escaping. Green roofs, or living roofs, can also provide insulation and they keep the building cool in summer, too. They are made of living vegetation, such as grass or a plant called sedum. Green roofs can encourage different animals to make their home there.

Solar panels

Green roof

2 🔊 2.17 **Listen and read**

Domotic houses

The word *domotic* is a contraction of two words: *domus/domo* (that's Latin for home) and *automatic*. Domotic houses have an automatic central system that you can use to control things at home. For example, the lighting, security, TV, heating, air conditioning, shutters, computer, refrigerator and other appliances. You can also control the watering of plants. Some experts think that in the future all our homes will be domotic, but, at the moment, the technology is new and very expensive. It will be years before we can all control our homes from one small box.

Control panel of a domotic house

3 🔊 **2.18 Speak, listen and read**

Skyscrapers

The word *skyscraper* appeared in the 1880s and it is still used today. It literally means that the building scrapes the sky. The invention of the telephone in 1876 and the electric lift in 1880 improved tall buildings drastically. People could live or work on the top floors of very tall buildings because it was easy to get there in lifts. Skyscrapers used a steel structure, telephones, lifts and central heating among other innovations.
See the height of some very interesting tall buildings on the graph.

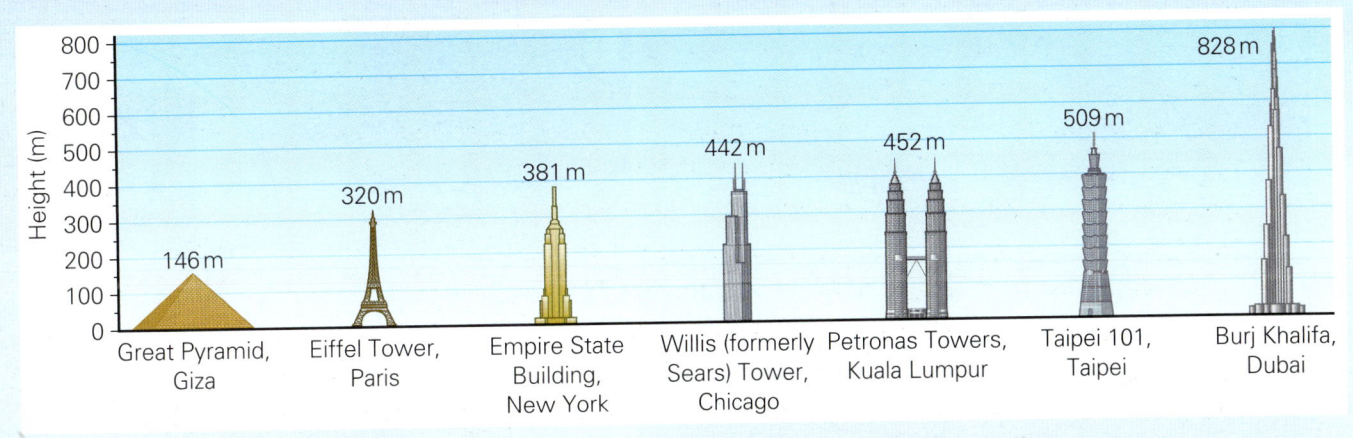

Building	Height
Great Pyramid, Giza	146 m
Eiffel Tower, Paris	320 m
Empire State Building, New York	381 m
Willis (formerly Sears) Tower, Chicago	442 m
Petronas Towers, Kuala Lumpur	452 m
Taipei 101, Taipei	509 m
Burj Khalifa, Dubai	828 m

4 🔊 **2.20 Listen and read**

Building with steel

Different materials can be used when building. Steel is a great material to build big structures because it is very strong. Steel is formed by mixing very hot molten iron with carbon. Iron is a chemical element, which means we find it in nature. We don't need a process to make iron. It is a strong, hard, heavy, grey metal. But steel is much stronger and more flexible than regular iron. This means that steel does not break easily. That is the reason why we often use steel instead of iron today. We use steel to make machines, cars, tools, buildings, knives and many other things. Since steel can melt under very high temperatures, the steel structure of a building must be protected from fire.

🌀 Super Tour 3

Choose one of the topics on pages 50–51. Find more information about it on the Internet and in books. Prepare a presentation with pictures for your classmates.

5 Language stop

1 🔊 2.21 **Listen and find three mistakes in the pictures. Speak**

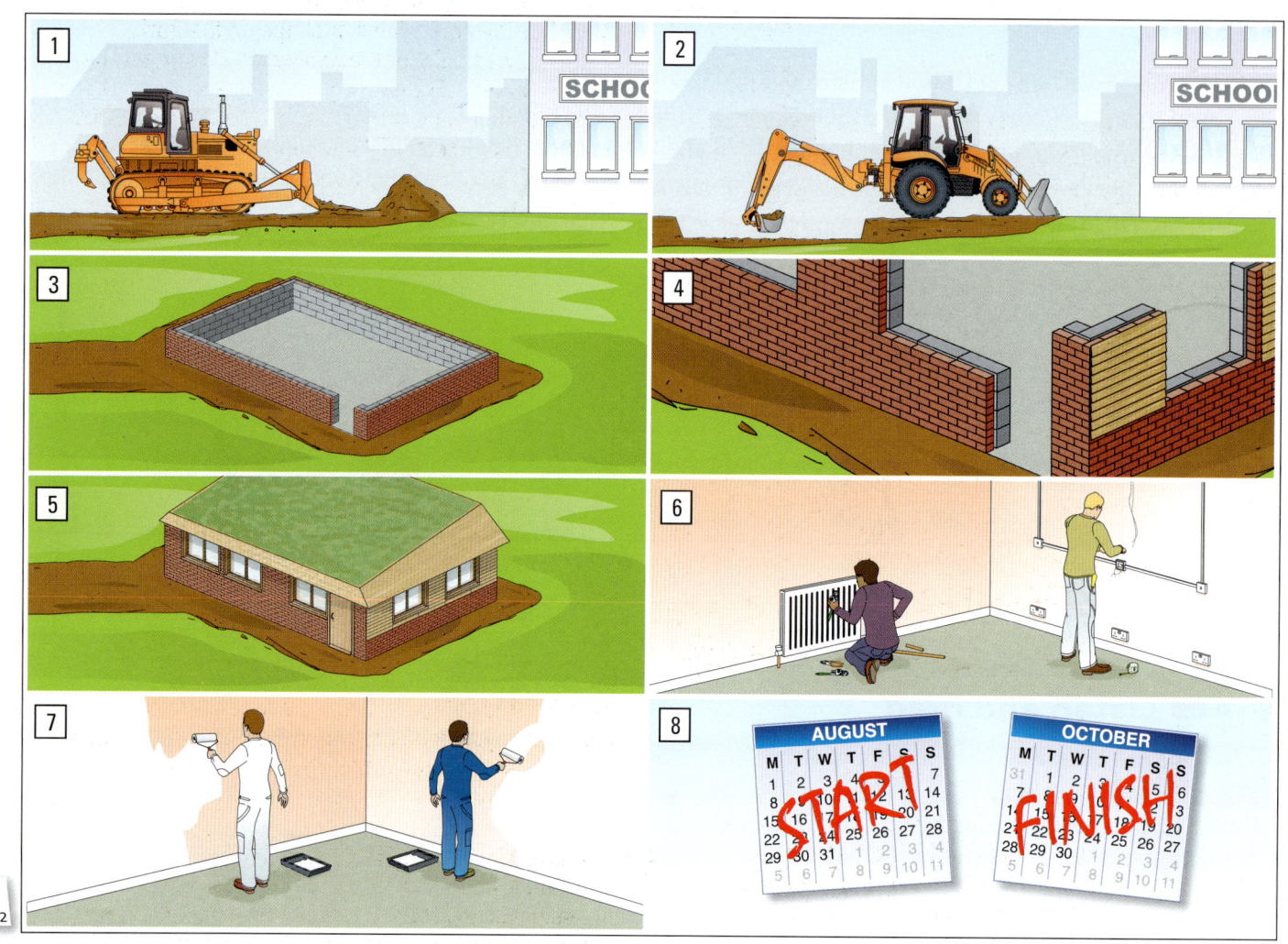

2 Read and answer

First, we**'ll** discuss the type of classroom we want.
Then an architect **will** design the classroom.
It **won't** be an eco-building.
The headteacher **will** contact the contractors.
Next, the contractors **will** calculate the cost for the headteacher. She**'ll** agree to pay for the work.
I**'ll** prepare a presentation for the school.
After that, the building work **will** start.
Finally, you**'ll** all come to the opening party.
Will our teacher like the classroom?

> 1 Look at the words in blue. What do they indicate? What is the negative form?
> 2 What form does the second verb take in these sentences?
> 3 What happens to *will* when it follows a subject pronoun? What happens in questions?

> 1 Look at the words in red. What do they indicate?
> 2 What words do you use in your language to express the same?

Super Tour 4

You and your classmates want to build a new classroom. Discuss your ideas and work together to draw a plan. Then explain what you will do and in what order.

Do you know that ...?

1 Read and find

2 🎧 2.22 Read and listen

1 The Taj Mahal, Agra, India
The Taj Mahal was built in the 17th century. Emperor Shah Jahan wanted a tomb for his wife Mumtaz Mahal, who died in childbirth. It is one of the most beautiful and romantic tombs in the world. The building is made of white marble that changes colour according to the weather and the time of the day. The emperor employed a group of architects to work on the design and construction of the building but he supervised their work. In 1983 the Taj Mahal became a UNESCO world heritage site.

2 The Rolex Learning Centre, Lausanne, Switzerland
This pioneer building is part of the Federal Polytechnic School in Lausanne. It opened in 2010 and the Japanese architectural group SAANA designed it. It is a library and learning centre for all the students at the polytechnic. This means that science, technology and architecture students can easily meet and share knowledge in the large open space created in the building. The circles in the roof, floor and walls represent the way humans move and help to create natural connections between the different areas of the building.

3 The Eiffel Tower, Paris, France
The Eiffel Tower is a familiar shape on the Paris skyline. It was built for the *Exposition Universelle* by Gustave Eiffel, a French engineer and architect. The Eiffel Tower opened on 6th May 1889. It is 300 metres tall, plus the 20-metre TV antenna on top. It is made of steel. The plan was to demolish the Eiffel Tower after 20 years, but it stayed because it was used for communication purposes after the exhibition. The first long-distance radio message was sent from the tower on 12th January 1908.

4 The Burj Khalifa, Dubai, United Arab Emirates
This amazing skyscraper gained the official title of 'Tallest Building in the World' in 2010 when it opened to the public. The architects were the firm SOM (Skidmore, Owings, Merrill) from Chicago. They are world experts in the design of tall buildings. The skyscraper is 828 metres high and there are flats, offices and a hotel inside it. It also has the highest swimming pool in the world.
The building can have about 35,000 people in it at the same time and its water system supplies about 946,000 litres a day. It uses a water condensation collection system that recycles the humid air outside to produce water for watering the plants.

5 The Tate Modern, London, England
The Tate Modern in London was once a power station but now it is an art gallery. It is a renovated building. This means that the architects started with the old building and worked with the original structure in their new design. They renovated the 4.2 million bricks, the windows and the 99-metre high chimney. They built two new floors along the top of the building, with floor to ceiling glass walls.
The architects were Swiss, Jacques Herzog and Pierre de Meuron. They won a competition to transform the power station into a new home for one of the most important collections of international modern art in the UK. They beat over 70 architects from around the world.

Super Tour 5
Look on the Internet and choose another interesting building, e.g. the Sydney Opera House. Find some interesting facts about it and write a short text.

5 SKILLS TICKET

1 🔊 2.23 Read

Mohawk steelworkers

by Emily Allen, architecture student

I feel terribly scared when I look at this picture. It was taken in 1932 by Charles C. Ebbets. The picture shows a group of workers having lunch on floor 69 of the building they were constructing. But there is nothing under their feet! Honestly, I do not want to imagine any of my friends or relatives in that situation. It is so extremely dangerous!

But who were these workers? Most of them were American Indians and, most commonly, from the Mohawk tribe. They were excellent iron- and steelworkers. The original homeland of the Mohawks was the region that extends from the north-east of New York State to the south of Canada. Many generations of Mohawks fished and hunted animals in those lands to live.

So how did they become so good at working with iron and steel? In the mid-1880s some Mohawks started working on the construction of a steel bridge over the St Lawrence River, near their homes in Canada. They were not trained to do the work, but their employers noticed that they seemed comfortable on the bridge that they were building. They were not scared of climbing and moving around high above the ground.

It was not easy to find workers who could work at such heights as it was dangerous. So their employers decided to train the Mohawks to work with iron and steel properly and see what happened.

The company trained the Mohawks to do skilled steelwork and the results were excellent. With the right tools the Mohawks did a fantastic job. From that moment, the Mohawks helped to build bridges and high buildings. They gained a good reputation as excellent steelworkers.

More than six generations of Mohawks have helped to build New York's highest skyscrapers and structures: the Chrysler Building, the George Washington Bridge, the Empire State Building, the Rockefeller Center, etc.

As skilled steelworkers, the Mohawks also helped in the general search after the Twin Towers of the World Trade Center came down in September 2001.

People call the Mohawks 'skywalkers' because they walk and work on thin steel structures, very high above city streets. But how do they feel? In interviews, the skywalkers say that they feel fear the same as everyone else, but they have a better way of dealing with it.

2 Read and answer

1 Who are the Mohawks?
2 Where did they live in the past?
3 What are they good at?
4 Who trained them?
5 What kind of buildings do they help to build?

6 Discovering New Zealand

In this unit you will
- learn about the culture, people and history of New Zealand as well as the geography, landscape and wildlife
- use the present and past continuous
- use this knowledge to plan a holiday to New Zealand and make a photo album

1 3.01 Read, listen and speak

Our New Zealand holiday list - things to do and find out!
- What's the capital city and where is it?
- What sea life can we see?
- What is special about Rotorua and the Waitomo Caves?
- Who lived in New Zealand before the Europeans arrived?
- Where did Peter Jackson film *The Lord of the Rings*?
- Where can we see the *haka*?

Geography New Zealand is a long, narrow country of about 700 islands situated in the South Pacific. The North and South Islands are the biggest and most important. The capital city, Wellington, is on the North Island but the biggest city there is Auckland. The biggest city on the South Island is Christchurch.
The landscape of New Zealand is incredible. There are high snowy mountains, glaciers, fjords, beaches, geysers, hot springs, rainforests and green countryside with unique plants and animals, both inland and in the sea. Look out for whales, dolphins, seals and a great variety of birds.

People The first Maori settlers in New Zealand arrived from Polynesia between AD 1000 and 1200. They did not have a written language but their culture was very rich. *Aotearoa* is their name for New Zealand. It means land of the long white cloud. The word *Maori* means local people. The first European to see New Zealand was Dutchman Abel Tasman in 1642 but he did not land on the islands. Then the British explorer Captain James Cook followed in 1769. Today, New Zealand is a bicultural society of Europeans and Maori. Approximately 15% of the total population is Maori and 50% of the whole population is under 36 years old.

6 Story

Captain Cook

2 🔊 3.02 Look, listen and read

1. James Cook was born in 1728 in a very small town in Yorkshire, in the north of England, not far from the sea. As a little boy he did farm work with his family and he also went to school. Then, at the age of 17, he became a shop assistant in a nearby fishing town.

2. James loved to go to the harbour and listen to the stories that the fishermen told about the sea. He also loved to watch the ships that were carrying coal to London and to read books about the great oceans of the world.

I'm working in a nice shop but it's not the place for me. I want to go to sea and visit faraway places.

3. A year later, he started work as an apprentice for John Walker, a coal ship owner. James helped to refit ships. But while he was working on the ships, he studied a lot. He taught himself algebra, geometry, trigonometry, navigation and astronomy.

This is what I need to know to command a ship.

4. James Cook became a sailor and he went on several sea voyages. In 1755, he joined the Royal Navy. He crossed the Atlantic Ocean several times and made detailed maps of the coastlines of different regions, such as Quebec and Newfoundland in Canada.

What's he doing?

He's drawing a map of the coast. He's very good at it. On our last voyage he was drawing charts and maps most of the time.

5. In 1768, the Royal Navy gave Cook command of the ship HMS *Endeavour* for a very special mission. There was a crew of 94 men on the ship. Some of them were important scientists.

We want you to go to Tahiti, in the Pacific Ocean, to observe the Transit of Venus.

This is when the planet Venus passes in front of the sun. The scientists on your ship can observe and measure the distance of the sun from the Earth.

Unit 6

But there was a secret reason for the expedition.

"We want you to find out if Terra Australis exists or not."

"Many people believe that Terra Australis is an undiscovered continent between Tahiti and New Zealand. Maybe we can claim new colonies where we can trade, find gold or send settlers."

(6)

HMS *Endeavour* left Plymouth, England, on 26th August 1768. She sailed west for eight months towards Brazil. After a difficult voyage from Brazil, the expedition arrived safely in Tahiti in April 1769. The scientists observed the Transit of Venus. Cook and his crew found that Tahitian people were very friendly.

"Have some of this."

"This is really nice. Thank you."

(7)

Tupaia, a Tahitian chief, spoke some English and wanted to join the expedition. He travelled with Cook when HMS *Endeavour* left Tahiti on 13th July 1769. Cook guided the ship towards the coasts of New Zealand in search of Terra Australis. Tupaia was a great companion. He explained the practices and customs of the native inhabitants of the islands they visited on the way.

"What are they making?"

"They're building a temple with lava rock."

(8)

James Cook and his crew were searching for Terra Australis but they did not find it.

"Where's Terra Australis?"

(9)

After sailing for three months, HMS *Endeavour* arrived in New Zealand, but the native people, the Maori, attacked the ship to defend their land. The attacks continued in other places on the coast where James Cook tried to stop.

(10)

57

6 Story

11 HMS *Endeavour* was navigating the northern tip of New Zealand when she encountered serious problems because of very strong winds. She was still trying to find a place to stop.

12 Finally, Cook found a safe place to land. He made good friends with the Maori there and traded with fish and fresh vegetables. Tupaia's language was very close to the Maori language, so he helped to communicate. The British visitors found that the plants, animals and customs of New Zealand were very different to those in England.

- Are you collecting samples of those strange plants?
- Yes, I am. There's nothing like this in England.

13 Cook made detailed records of what he saw and learnt about New Zealand. He also created a map of the coastline. His map showed that New Zealand had two islands, but it did not show Terra Australis.

14 HMS *Endeavour* left New Zealand on 31st March 1770. She went to the east coast of Australia and then back to England, via the Cape of Good Hope, South Africa. The ship arrived home in July 1771. Captain James Cook's expedition was a success.

- Congratulations! You observed the Transit of Venus and collected an incredible number of new botanical and zoological specimens.
- Now we've got maps of New Zealand and the east coast of Australia and we can claim those countries for King George III of England. You're promoted to Commander!

15 Cook returned to New Zealand two more times in command of HMS *Resolution*, in 1773 and 1777. On 14th February 1779, Cook was killed in an argument in Hawaii. His explorations and his maps were a great contribution to humanity.

Unit 6

3 🔊 3.02 Listen and speak. How much can you say about each of these?

1 James Cook's youth
2 Cook's studies and early career 
3 Captain Cook's maps of the world 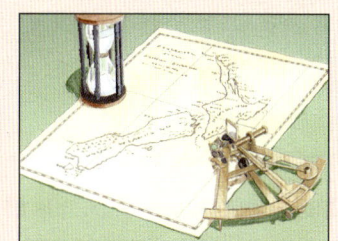
4 The journey of HMS *Endeavour* 
5 The Maori 
6 Tupaia 
7 Terra Australis 
8 The Transit of Venus 

4 Play a team game and get to New Zealand first

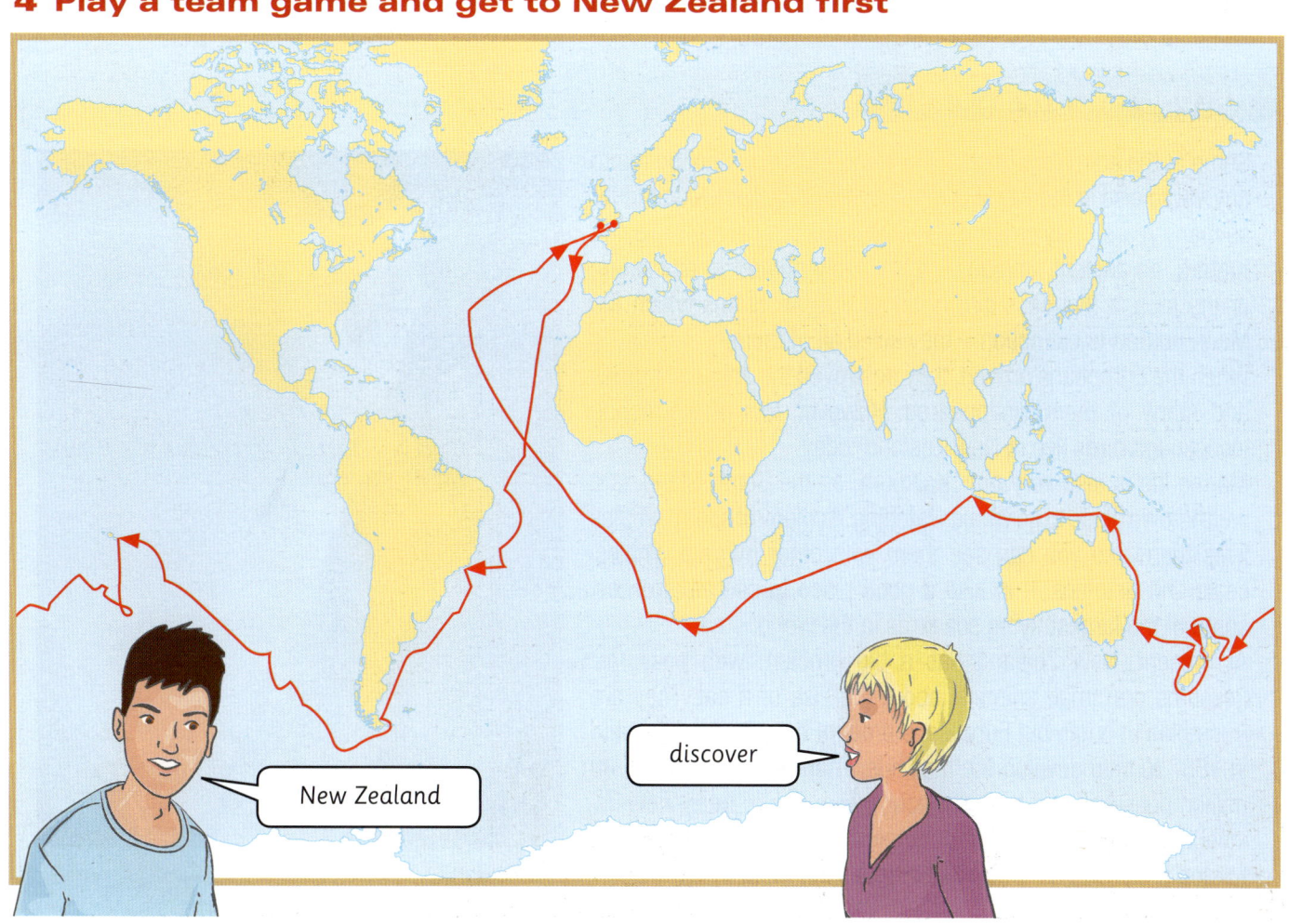

New Zealand

discover

6 About New Zealand

1 🔊 3.03 **Listen, read and speak**

Travel New Zealand

THE TREATY OF WAITANGI

Following Captain Cook's detailed report on the islands of New Zealand, European settlers, mainly British, started to go there. In the 19th century, the British had lots of colonies – countries and islands around the world that belonged to them – and they wanted to make New Zealand a colony, too. The Treaty of Waitangi was a document that the British and some Maori chiefs signed in 1840. The idea was to give the Maori the same rights and the same amount of land as the Europeans who went there. But the question was, and still is, *what exactly did they sign?* The treaty is in two languages, Maori and English, but the two versions have different meanings. This meant that the Maori understood the treaty differently and they lost land that they wanted to keep. Today people think that the Treaty of Waitangi is the document which founded New Zealand and Waitangi Day – 6th February – is a public holiday.

Maori chief signing the treaty

NATURE AND WILDLIFE

Some of the animals and plants in New Zealand cannot be found anywhere else in the world because the islands were isolated for so many years. They are thousands of years old. For example, the tuatara, an ancient, unique reptile closely related to dinosaurs; or the moa, a flightless bird of about 200 kilograms which the Maori hunted to extinction – they killed all of them.

When the Europeans arrived, they destroyed the animals' homes and many of them disappeared. However, lots of interesting insects and birds live in New Zealand today.

Marine life is also very rich. Kaikoura, on the South Island, is a well-known place to go whale watching. A colony of sperm whales lives there and you can see them with other migrant whales, seals and dolphins. It is also a good place to see albatrosses, some of the largest flying sea birds in the world.

At present, New Zealand has a big problem with possums. Possums are small animals, about the size of a cat. They are Australian in origin but Europeans brought them to New Zealand in 1837 to help develop the fur trade. There are now around 30 million possums and they are eating everything: trees, flowers, insects, birds and eggs. Unfortunately there is no natural predator to stop the possums – no other animals eat them.

A possum

Unit 6

SPORTS

All sorts of outdoor sports and activities are possible in the varied landscape of New Zealand, for example, sailing, rowing and snow sports such as skiing and snowboarding. The narrow gorges in the mountains in the interior of the country are ideal for whitewater rafting, kayaking or jetboating. Other adventure and high-risk sports such as skydiving or bungee jumping are also very popular. The world's first commercial bungee jump was established in 1986 on the Kawarau Bridge near Queenstown, on the South Island, and there are now lots of other bungee sites in the area.

But the national sport in New Zealand is rugby. The country's national rugby team, the All Blacks, have an incredible success record. They always perform a *haka* before a match. A *haka* is a Maori dance used to welcome or to scare visitors. The dancers slap their thighs and chests, enlarge their eyes and stick out their tongues. New Zealand-born Charles Munro first introduced rugby to his home country in the 1860s after he watched a game when he was studying in London.

Bungee jumping

*The All Blacks performing a **haka***

Super Tour 1

Talk to your classmates about which sport you would like to try and why. Then find out more about the sport on the Internet. Where can you do it in New Zealand? Can you do it in your country, too?

6 Language stop

1 🔊 3.04 Listen, read and answer

Holidays in New Zealand
Day 1: Flying from London Heathrow
Wow, it's fantastic! **I'm travelling** to New Zealand! **I'm sitting** in the plane by a window. The plane **is taking** off. Mum and Dad **are sitting** next to me. The seats are very comfortable. The flight will take around 27 hours with one stop in Los Angeles, on the west coast of the USA. Now **we're crossing** the Atlantic Ocean. **I'm looking** through the window and all I can see are clouds and the sea. Mum and Dad **are watching** a film. Some people **are listening** to music and the young woman sitting in front of me **is reading** some leaflets about New Zealand. Perhaps **she's planning** what to visit. **I'm not doing** any of those activities. Mum asks me, 'Laura, you **are concentrating** very hard. What **are** you **writing**?' '**I'm writing** my diary. I want to keep a record of everything we do in New Zealand!' I say. 'Well, have a break now! The flight attendant **is coming**. **She's serving** lunch!' Mum says.

1 Look at each set of verbs in blue. Is Laura describing a routine or something that is happening now? How do you know?
2 How many verbs are there in each set?
3 Which verb is always there? What do you add to the second verb?
4 Find these verbs: *write, come, serve, travel, sit, plan, cross*. What do you notice about the spelling of the verbs? Can you find a rule?

2 🔊 3.05 Listen, look and answer

Laura is showing her friend Katie some pictures of her holidays in New Zealand.
Laura New Zealand is a fantastic country. Look at these pictures!
Katie Who's that?
Laura That's Mum. She **was swimming** in a warm water lake. Dad **wasn't swimming** … he hates the water! And look at this one. Mum and Dad **were looking** at an enormous glacier. It's the Franz Josef glacier in the Southern Alps – really high mountains on the South Island.
Katie I can't see you in this picture.
Laura We were on another boat. Our boat **was sailing** behind the boat in the photo so you can't see us. We **were watching** whales.
Katie And what **were** you **doing** in this picture?
Laura I **was** just **taking** the picture of the sky tower. We **were visiting** Auckland, the biggest city in New Zealand, and we **were waiting** to go inside.

1 Is this text about the present or the past? How do you know?
2 Compare the verbs in this text with the verbs in the text above. What is different? What is the same?

Super Tour 2

Make a photo album of your last holiday and write what you and your family were doing in each photo.

Do you know that ...?

1 🔊 3.06 **Listen and find the best heading**

- The country of sheep and cows
- Another kiwi
- A bird as the national symbol
- New Zealand's wonders
- Historic sights to visit

2 🔊 3.06 **Read and listen**

1 The oldest building in New Zealand is a wooden house called the Kerikeri Mission House, in the town of Kerikeri on the North Island. The Church Missionary Society built the house for a priest around 1822. Later, James Kemp, the town's storekeeper, lived in the house. He also built the Stone Store in 1832, now the oldest stone building in New Zealand, next to his house.

2 New Zealand had no predatory animals before humans arrived there, so some birds lived on the ground. Their wings became very small and they could not fly. This is true of the kiwi, New Zealand's most famous bird. Kiwis are about the size of a chicken and are nocturnal, flightless birds. They lay very big eggs, about 20% of their body weight, and have long beaks and hair-like feathers. They eat worms, insects and leaves. Kiwi is a Maori word that comes from the cry the male kiwi makes. The bird is New Zealand's national symbol. People also use the nickname 'Kiwi' to talk about New Zealanders, though many New Zealanders have never seen a kiwi bird.

3 Captain Cook brought the first sheep to New Zealand in 1773. In the middle of the 19th century, British colonists successfully introduced sheep farming. Until 1940 New Zealand exported most of the meat and wool from its sheep to the UK. Today New Zealand has 40 million sheep and eight million cows. That represents ten sheep and two cows for every person that lives in the country.

4 The kiwi fruit is native of China. New Zealand introduced the first kiwi seeds in 1906 and collected the first fruit in 1910. First they called it the 'Chinese gooseberry', but when New Zealand started to export the fruit, they decided to change the name to kiwi fruit.

5 Rotorua is in the centre of the North Island. When you arrive in the town, you will notice the smell of rotten eggs. This is because of the minerals and amazing geothermal activity in the area. There are lakes of hot water, boiling mud pools, geysers and hot springs. When you see all these things, you soon forget the smell! Not far from Rotorua are the enormous Waitomo Caves with beautiful stalactites on the cave roof and stalagmites on the floor. The caves are all dark except for the Glow-worm Grotto. This cave is full of glow-worms, small insects which glow and light up the cave with their tiny clear lights.

6 SKILLS TICKET

1 🔊 3.08 Read

Famous New Zealanders

Sir Edmund Hillary 
Edmund Hillary was born in Auckland, on the North Island of New Zealand, in 1919 and he died there in 2008. Hillary was one of the most famous mountain climbers in the world. When he was 16, he went on a skiing trip to the Southern Alps, on New Zealand's South Island. There he saw snow for the first time and it was on this trip that he became interested in mountain climbing. Hillary climbed his first mountain, Mount Ollivier (1,933 metres) in the Southern Alps, in 1939.

Hillary joined the Royal New Zealand Air Force as a navigator during World War II, but he returned to New Zealand and to mountain climbing after the war. He reached the summit of the highest mountain in the Southern Alps, Aoraki/Mount Cook (3,754 metres), in 1947. Then he started to climb mountains outside of New Zealand, in the Swiss and Austrian Alps, and finally in the Himalayas.

From 1921–1952 eight expeditions attempted to climb the highest mountain in the world, Mount Everest (8,848 metres) on the Nepal-Tibet border, but all failed. In 1953 Hillary joined a British expedition and he and his Nepalese Sherpa, Tenzing Norgay, reached the summit on 29th May at 11:30 am.

The King or Queen of England is also the head of New Zealand and news of the expedition's success reached London on 2nd June, the day of the coronation of Queen Elizabeth II. Hillary was knighted – he became Sir Edmund Hillary – that same year and Tenzing Norgay received The British Empire Medal.

Sir Peter Jackson 
Peter Jackson was born near Wellington in 1961 and still lives in New Zealand. He is one of the world's most successful film directors. Jackson was an only child and he loved to watch television programmes and films with special effects. *King Kong* was his favourite. When he watched the sad story about the giant gorilla, he knew he wanted to become a film director.

He was nine years old when he started to make his own short films with his family's video camera. At 16 he made *Bad Taste*, his first short horror fantasy film with neighbours and friends as actors.

Jackson later discovered J.R.R. Tolkien's *The Lord of the Rings*. The three-volume book fascinated him and he started to film the trilogy in 1999. The first part, *The Fellowship of the Ring*, hit the cinemas two years later. The following two parts, *The Two Towers* and *The Return of the King*, came out in 2002 and 2003. Jackson filmed the whole trilogy in New Zealand, in more than 150 locations, including Queenstown and the Southern Alps. The three films won a total of 17 Oscars, including the best picture and the best director.

Jackson's remake of the film *King Kong*, which he loved as a child, was one of the most successful films of the year 2005. Jackson was knighted in 2009 and is still making films.

2 Read and answer
1 When did Edmund Hillary first become interested in mountain climbing?
2 Why is 29th May 1953 an important date?
3 How long did it take the news to reach London?
4 Why was the film *King Kong* important in Peter Jackson's life?
5 When did the film *The Fellowship of the Ring* come out?

TOP DECK RACE

1. What town did the volcano Mount Vesuvius bury in AD 79?
2. Where was Paul Klee born?
3. Which is the largest art museum in the world?
4. Who was the first woman pharaoh?
5. Which is the longest river in the world?
6. Where is most of the Earth's water?
7. How much of the Earth's water does the farming industry use?
8. Where is the Taj Mahal?
9. What is the Maori name for New Zealand?
10. Who was the first European man to land on New Zealand?

1. Where is Mount Vesuvius?
2. Can you name a famous Cubist painter?
3. Where can you see the painting *Mona Lisa*?
4. Where is the River Nile?
5. Who was Cleopatra?
6. Why are glaciers melting?
7. When did the Empire State Building open?
8. Which is the tallest building in the world?
9. Who were the first inhabitants of New Zealand?
10. What is the name of the document that founded New Zealand?

Do you know that ...?

1 Read and speak

1

Mandarin Chinese   *Portuguese*   *English*   *Korean*
Arabic   *Russian*   *Swedish*   *Hindi*
Japanese   *Spanish*   *French*   *German*

People speak around 6,500 different languages in the world today. The four languages spoken by the largest number of people as their first language are: Mandarin Chinese with around 873 million speakers, Hindi with 370 million, Spanish with 350 million and English with 340 million speakers.

English is the language most people speak as a second language.
About 2,000 languages have fewer than 1,000 speakers. Some of these languages are in danger of dying out. Around 70 languages disappeared in the 20th century and five have disappeared so far in the 21st century.

2

Vitáme vás — Välkommen — Vitajte
Witamy — Bienvenido — Bienvenu
Bem-vindo — Willkommen — Welcome

People speak around 225 different languages in Europe. Some of these languages are official languages of a country and others are official languages of a region, while some are minority languages which certain groups of people speak. Most European countries have two or more official languages.
The five European languages spoken by the largest number of people as their first language are: Russian (150 million), German (95 million), English, French (65 million each) and Italian (60 million).
56% of Europeans speak another language as well as their first language. Switzerland has four national languages. English is the most popular second language in Europe.

3

European Day of Languages   *Europäischer Tag der Sprachen*
Día Europeo de las Lenguas
Journée européenne des langues   *Giornata europea delle lingue*

Europe celebrates the European Day of Languages on 26th September. The Council of Europe started the day in 2001 to encourage language learning across Europe. The Council of Europe wanted to increase multilingualism and improve intercultural understanding. Schools from different countries celebrate the day by making posters, learning words or singing songs in different languages, sending postcards to other schools, etc.

European Day of Languages

2 🔊 **1.37 Listen and speak. How do you say 'Hello' and 'Goodbye'?**

1. 'Hei' 'Näkemiin'
2. 'Hola' 'Adiós'
3. 'Cześć' 'Do widzenia'
4. 'Ciao' 'Arrivederci'
5. 'Bonjour' 'Au revoir'

3 🔊 **1.38 Sing the song**

Witamy. Vitáme vás. Vitajte.
Bienvenido. Bienvenu. Bem-vindo.
Välkommen. Willkommen. Welcome
To the European Day of Languages!
Whoever you are,
Wherever you live,
Whatever language you speak,
Let's celebrate together,
The European Day of Languages!
Let's celebrate the day forever.

Do you know that ...?

1 Read and speak

1

New moon — Full moon

The date of the Chinese New Year changes from year to year, but it always takes place between 21st January and 19th February. The Chinese calendar is a lunar calendar, which means that each month begins with the new moon and ends with the full moon.
The New Year celebrations begin at midnight with the new moon on the first day of the first month in the Chinese calendar and end with the full moon 15 days later. The last day of the New Year celebrations is the Lantern Festival. People celebrate it at night with music and dancing in the streets, which are decorated with lanterns. China is not the only country to celebrate Chinese New Year. Chinese people living in big cities around the world celebrate this festival, too.

2 Before the New Year, Chinese people clean their houses from top to bottom to wash away any bad luck. They also paint doors and windows, usually red, and decorate them with red and gold paper with messages of happiness and good health.

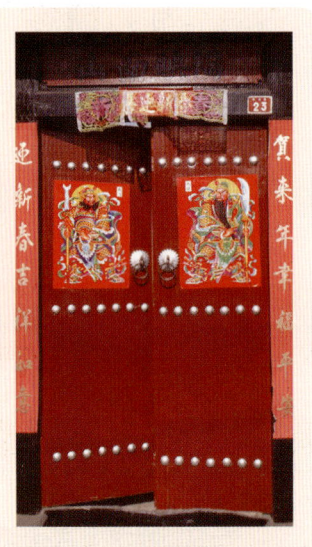

3 The dragon is a popular symbol of Chinese New Year. One of the main events is the Dragon Dance – a large procession through the streets with a dragon at the front. A group of dancers carries the dragon and moves it up and down. The Dragon Dance scares away evil spirits.

4 The Chinese calendar has a twelve-year cycle and each year has the name of an animal. A Chinese legend says that Chinese gods invited 12 animals to represent the years. The animals had a race. The rat was the winner so the first year in the cycle is the year of the rat. The rest of the years correspond to the order each animal finished the race: the rat, the ox, the tiger, the rabbit, the dragon, the snake, the horse, the sheep, the monkey, the rooster, the dog and the pig.

Chinese New Year

2 Play a game. Find the name of the year on the Chinese calendar

The ninth of February two thousand and five.

It's in the year of the rooster.

3 Read and find out

Some people believe that people born in a particular animal year have some of the characteristics of that animal.

Rat	The rat is clever, hardworking and a good friend, but gets bored easily.
Ox	The ox is hardworking, patient, kind and a bit shy.
Tiger	The tiger has a strong personality. It likes adventure, but doesn't like taking orders.
Rabbit	The rabbit is honest, friendly and a bit shy.
Dragon	The dragon is generous, full of energy and loves freedom.
Snake	The snake is patient, generous and has a good sense of humour.
Horse	The horse is very hardworking, independent and enjoys travelling.
Sheep	The sheep loves beautiful things, but is shy and doesn't like arguments.
Monkey	The monkey is very clever and creative.
Rooster	The rooster is independent, punctual and hardworking.
Dog	The dog is a good friend, generous and kind.
Pig	The pig is honest, but a bit untidy at home.

Do you know that...?

Earth Day

1 🔊 2.24 **Look, listen and read**

1. In 1963 in the USA, industries often polluted the air with huge black clouds of toxic gases. They polluted the rivers and oceans with toxic waste and garbage. There were no laws to protect the environment.

2. Many people were worried about the future of the Earth. Senator Nelson, a politician, was one of them.

- The Earth gives us so much and we seem to just give back waste.
- Yes, the Earth is our home but we are destroying it. We must do something about it.

3. The senator shared his worries about the environment with other politicians and with other people in the country, but the results were not very good. Then in 1969 he had an idea.

- We must have a special day to teach everybody about the environment and how to protect it.
- Excellent idea, but how are we going to do it? How are we going to get people involved?

4. First we must contact schools and communities. We'll ask them to identify environmental problems in their communities and to plan activities to solve them. Then, on the special day, they'll carry out the activities to show their concern for their environment.

5. The first Earth Day was celebrated on April 22, 1970. About 20 million people in the USA made promises to help the environment. The idea was a great success because people of all ages participated with their own initiatives. Since then, on April 22, Earth Day is celebrated in many countries around the world. India, for example, celebrated Earth Day in 2010 in 17 cities through Mother Earth concerts, community service and tree-planting projects. Many schools worldwide celebrate Earth Day by organizing petition letter writing to politicians, contests (poster, essay, slogans, eARTh, songs, poems, etc), green parades, 'Environmental Hero' awards, Council of All Beings, recycling or energy fairs, etc.

Earth Day

2 Speak and read

What happened after April 22, 1970 in the USA?
They created a special agency to protect the environment. They introduced different laws, for example the Clean Air Act, and in the next three years they introduced the Clean Water Act, the Endangered Species Act and the Resource Conservation and Recovery Act.
Other countries developed similar acts.
But the job is not complete. Global warming and other issues are very important now.

3 Photography contest: Speak and choose

1

Beauty is beauty. *By Adam Woods, 13.*

2

Amazing mountains. *By Alice Smith, 14.*

3

Wonderful stream to daydream. *By Liz Richards, 13.*

4

The sun is the solution! *By Anne Farwell, 13.*

Macmillan Education
Between Towns Road, Oxford OX4 3PP
A division of Macmillan Publishers Limited
Companies and representatives throughout the world

ISBN 978-0-230-41216-3

Text © María José Lobo, Pepita Subirà 2011
Design and illustration © Macmillan Publishers Limited 2011

First published 2011

All rights reserved; no part of this publication may be reproduced, stored in a retrieval system, transmitted in any form, or by any means, electronic, mechanical, photocopying, recording, or otherwise, without the prior written permission of the publishers.

Designed by Greenbird Design
Illustrated by Vladimir Aleksic, Ilias Arahovitis, John Dillow, Martin Sanders, Pete Smith, ODI, Red Giraffe, Gary Wing
Cover design by Greenbird Design
Cover photographs from Alamy/Keith Morris, Getty/Jerry Driendl, Photolibrary/PureStock.

Authors' acknowledgements
We would like to thank Ursula Bader, Brigitte Ruhstaller and Heidi Zumstein for their great initiative, commitment, encouragement and support; for their firm beliefs and for their ambition to make the teaching and learning of English an effective and memorable experience for everyone.
We would also like to thank Susan Sharp and the whole team at Macmillan Education for their huge involvement and excellent work, and our families for their constant understanding.
None of this would have been possible without them.

The publishers would like to thank all those who commented on the syllabus and materials for *Top deck 2* and provided feedback, in particular Dorothea Fuchs and Françoise Hänggi for piloting individual units of *Top deck 2*. We also thank all those who have let us into their classrooms to research this course.

The authors and publishers would like to thank the following for permission to reproduce their photographs:

Akg-images p11(br), akg-images/De Agostini Picture Library p25(t,b), akg-images/ullstein bild p23(tr), akg-images/Gerard Degeorge p33 (bcl);akg-images/Alfio Garozzo p5(t), akg-images/Rainer Hackenberg p11(tc), akg-images/Erich Lessing p33(tl), akg-images /James Morris p3(t), Akg images Succession Picasso/© Succession Picasso/DACS, London 2011 p21, akg-images/Dr. E. Strouhal p33(bm);
Alamy/John Elk III p63(tl), Alamy/Clynt Garnham Architecture p51, Alamy/icpix_hk p68(t) Alamy/imagebroker p50(c), Alamy/ImageDJ p63(cr), Alamy/Lebrecht Music and Arts Photo Library p19(r), Alamy/Mary Evans Picture Library;
Ardea.com/Steffen & Alexandra Sailer p60(b);
Ark Religion/Helene Rogers p33(cm);
Brandx p30 (br, bl), p32, p71(3);
The Bridgeman Art Library/Marcus (20th century)/Alexander Turnbull Library, Wellington, New Zealand p60(t);
Corbis p71(1), Corbis/Pallava Bagla p39(l), Corbis/DENIS BALIBOUSE/Reuters p53(e), Corbis/Heide Benser p35(l), Corbis/Bettman p23(br), Corbis/Bettmann p54(l), Corbis/Peter Foley p24(b), Corbis/Gianni Dagli Ortti p31, Corbi p43(cr), Corbis/José Fuste Raga p63(tr), Corbis/David Gubernick/AgStock Images p43(cr), Corbis/G Richardson/Robert Harding World Imagery p41(b), Corbis/Araldo de Lucs p13 (t), Corbis/Will & Deni McIntyre p43(tr), Corbis/Pinto p45(t), (b), Corbis/Sandro Vannini p33 (cl), Corbis/So Hing-Keung p68(cr), Corbis/Steven Vidler/Eurasia Press p61(t), Corbis/Steven Vidler/Eurasia Press p63(cl);
DigitalStock/Corbis p53(a);
Ecoscene/Chinch Gryniewicz p50(t);
Getty p11 (tl, bl), pp15 (tcl), 33(br) p70(t), p71(2), Getty Images p64(r), Getty Images/AFP p30 (c), Getty Images/AFP p61(b), Getty Images/Bloomberg p53(b), Getty Images/National Geographic p63(br), Getty Images/Frank Rothe p15(t,b), Getty Images/Paul Giamou p49, Getty Images/Frans Lemmens p43(br), Getty Images/Gjon Mili/Contributor p24(t), Getty Images/Photodisc p5(br), Getty Images/Stringer p13(c);
Goodshoot p53(c);
Macmillan New Zealand p71(4);
Nature Picture Library p35(t), (b), Naturepl.com/Photo Resource Hawaii p13(bl);
www.paulkleezentrum.ch, Standardkunstler, Ida Maria und Hans Wilhelm Klee, Obstbergweg6, Bern 12,8 x 9 cm Zentrum Paul Klee, Bern, Klee Family Donation p19 (l), www.paulkleezentrum.ch, DACS 2010, Paul Klee Hauser am Meer, 1920, 134 Houses by the sea watercolour on paper on cardboard 24 x 32 cm Privatbesitz Schweiz p20(b);
Photodisc p67;
Photolibrary/Guido Alberto Rossi p5(bl),/Daniel Bergmann p13(br), Photolibrary/Adrian Houston p53(d), Photolibrary/Javier Larrea p50(b), Photolibrary/Doug Pearson p11(tr), Photolibrary/JTB Photo p15(bcl);
Pixtal p29;
Rex Features/N.Tepper/Arcaid p55 (t, b);
Reuters/Bogdan Cristel p55(cr);
Robert Harding/Derek Furlong p41(t);
Scala, Florence p20(t), Scala, Florence/The Museum of Modern Art, New York p20(m), Scala, Florence/The National Gallery, London p23(bl), Scala,Florence/© Succession Picasso/DACS, London 2011 p15(bcr);
Science Photo Library/Scott Camazine p43(cl), Science Photo Library/Worldsat International p35(r);
Still Pictures/sinopictures/Readfoto/Suichu Ru p68(cl)
Stockbyte p66 (5 flags);
TopFoto/The Granger Collection p64(l);
WaterAid/Anna Kari p39(r).

The authors and publishers are grateful to WaterAid, who kindly advised on the story *A visit to a water project*, pp36–38. Find out more about their work at www.wateraid.org.

These materials may contain links for third party websites. We have no control over, and are not responsible for, the contents of such third party websites. Please use care when accessing them.

Although we have tried to trace and contact copyright holders before publication, in some cases this has not been possible. If contacted we will be pleased to rectify any errors or omissions at the earliest opportunity.

Printed and bound in Spain by Edelvives

2016 2015 2014 2013 2012 2011
10   9   8   7   6   5   4   3   2   1